Programming in C++

by

Mark Walmsley

**BERNARD BABANI (publishing) LTD
THE GRAMPIANS
SHEPHERDS BUSH ROAD
LONDON W6 7NF
ENGLAND**

D1438341

PLEASE NOTE

Although every care has been taken with the production of this book to ensure that any projects, designs, modifications and/or programs, etc., contained herewith, operate in a correct and safe manner and also that any components specified are normally available in Great Britain, the Publishers and Author(s) do not accept responsibility in any way for the failure (including fault in design) of any project, design, modification or program to work correctly or for damage caused to any equipment that it may be connected to or used in conjunction with, or in respect of any other damage or injury that may be so caused, nor do the Publishers accept responsibility in any way for the failure to obtain specified components.

Notice is also given that if equipment that is still under warranty is modified in any way or used or connected with home-built equipment then that warranty may be void.

British Library Cataloguing in Publication Data:
A catalogue record for this book is available from the British Library

ISBN 0 85934 435 5

Cover Design by Gregor Arthur
Cover illustration by Adam Willis
Printed and bound in Great Britain by Cox & Wyman Ltd, Reading

ABOUT THIS BOOK

This book provides an introduction to the C++ programming language and its use in the design of object oriented software. The book is aimed at anyone interested in learning about C++ and object oriented programming but should be particularly useful for those wishing to rapidly acquire a good understanding of the language and start writing C++ programs. No prior knowledge of C++ (or indeed C) is assumed although a general background in computing will be helpful — the presentation is pyramidal in structure with early chapters laying the foundations for those that follow. Each new concept is fully explained with the help of line-drawings and illustrative coding examples.

Following a general introduction in chapter 1 the book is divided into three parts:

I. Basic Language Features (chapters 2 to 5)
II. Classes and Objects (chapters 6 to 10)
III. Advanced Language Features (chapters 11 to 15)

The first part discusses C++ data types, expressions, statements and functions. Classes form the basis for all object oriented facilities available in the C++ language — the second part of the book covers constructors and destructors, regular classes, operator overloading and dynamic objects. The final part of the book examines the different sorts of class provided by C++ (concrete, template, inheritable, interface and exception) and details their uses. The coverage throughout is broad rather than deep — many esoteric details are omitted for the sake of clarity.

The book contains numerous coding examples and several fully developed C++ classes — these can be modified to form the basis of a personalized C++ software library. All the code has been compiled and tested under Microsoft's Visual C++ (version 4.0) — no Microsoft specific extensions are assumed and the software should work with any compiler conforming to the current ANSI standard for the C++ language.

ABOUT THE AUTHOR

Mark Walmsley first discovered his interest in computing in the early 80s after reading a book on COBOL — he was soon writing programs in BASIC and shortly afterwards learnt about Z80 machine code. Over the last fifteen years he has gained considerable software development experience working with assembly code (for Z80, 68000 and 80x86 processors) and high-level languages (Pascal, FORTRAN, C, C++ and Java) — he is equally familiar with both UNIX and Windows operating systems. Along the way he graduated first from Durham University and then from York University gaining degrees in Mathematics and Electronic Engineering — he eventually returned to Durham to study for a PhD in Computational Physics and there he was involved in developing simulation software for modelling electronic components. More recently his days are devoted to the twin pursuits of designing multi-player computer games and writing books on computer programming.

CONTENTS

1. Overview of the C++ Language

The C++ programming language was originally conceived by Bjarne Stroustrup as an extension of the popular C language that would provide support for object oriented design. The C++ language started life as "C with Classes" and only later received its present name — the increment operator ++ denotes that C++ is something more than C. Indeed C++ inherits many of its features from C. It has a small number of intrinsic data types and programming constructs but complex data structures and processing algorithms can be built by combining the basic elements. Furthermore, both C and C++ provide a plentiful supply of operators for data manipulation. In fact, the main addition to C found in C++ is the class mechanism. Each C++ class defines a collection of objects all with similar characteristics, and every C++ object belongs to some class. Thus C++ classes underlie all of the object oriented facilities available in C++. An effective use of C++ consequently demands a good understanding of the base language shared with C and in addition a familiarity with the concepts of object oriented programming (OOP). This chapter presents an overview of C++ as an object oriented programming language, chapters 2 to 5 cover the basic language features and chapters 6 to 10 discuss C++ classes and objects. Finally, chapters 11 to 15 outline the mechanisms provided by C++ to assist in the design of software that can easily be reused in new projects with little or no modification. The production of reusable software is an excellent reason for adopting an object oriented approach to software design.

1.1 The C++ Programming Language

A C++ program consists of a sequence of program statements ordered from top to bottom. The C++ language is free-format so that the text of the various statements may (with a few restrictions) be laid out in a fashion that best emphasizes the function of the code. In particular, extra spaces, blank lines and comments can be added where necessary and a semi-colon (;) is used to mark the end of a statement. Each program statement performs one of three basic operations:

1. To specify structure or format
2. To allocate storage space
3. To process data

For every piece of data processed by the program, these three operations must be performed in sequence. Firstly, a data structure may be specified by a statement such as:

```
struct DATE {
    int Day;
    int Month;
    int Year;
};
```

Here a DATE structure is declared as consisting of three integers (int) which indicate the day, month and year. Of course, the C++ language itself defines the structure of some basic data types (such as int) to serve as building blocks for other data types. To allocate storage space for two data items, one of the basic type int and another of the user-defined type DATE, requires a pair of statements such as:

```
int count;
DATE today;
```

These statements create variables with the names count and today as shown in the figure below:

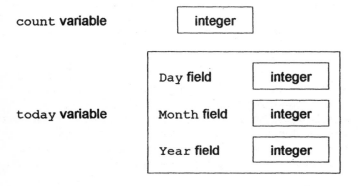

The variables can now hold data of the relevant type and be assigned values in subsequent data processing statements. For example, after the statement:

```
count = 10;
```

the variable count holds the value 10. This value may be modified as the count variable is processed further. To define a constant piece of data requires a statement such as:

```
const int TEN = 10;
```

A typical C++ program also defines a collection of functions to process its data. A function in C++ is a modular piece of code which accepts data in the form of variables and constants, performs various calculations using these parameters and finally returns a result. The format of the parameters passed to a function must be specified by some program statement that precedes the first use of the function to process data. For example, the following statement declares the Weekday() function as accepting a single parameter of type DATE and returning an integer result:

```
int Weekday(DATE);
```

The function calculates which day of the week corresponds to its parameter and returns a coded result: Sunday - 0, Moday - 1, ... , Saturday - 6. The important point to note is that this function declaration statement must precede any data processing statement such as:

```
count = Weekday(today);
```

This statement invokes the Weekday() function by passing it the value of the today variable and then stores the result calculated by the function in the count variable. The processing statements actually executed by the Weekday() function must also be defined somewhere. A matching pair of braces { } are used to enclose these statements — an

3

example of the syntax follows:

```
int Weekday(DATE date) {
     .
     .
  // perform processing here
     .
     .
}
```

This introduction to the C++ language is expanded in chapters 2 to 5.

1.2 Objects and Classes

In object oriented programming a problem is solved by identifying the essential ingredients of the problem and defining various object types to represent these concepts. The interaction of the objects then models the original problem and a solution may be expressed in natural terms. The previous section looked at C++ constants and variables for basic and structured types. The C++ language provides built-in support for processing data of basic types — for example, the arithmetic operations on integers (such as addition or multiplication) form an intrinsic part of the C++ language. Objects in C++ allow the same sort of capabilities to be provided for structured data types that are user-defined. In other words, a C++ object comprises two elements:

1. Structured data
2. Functions for manipulating this data

As an example, the C++ language provides an operator ++ which can be used to increment the value of an integer. An analogous operation could be defined for a DATE object by extending the structured data type DATE of section 1.1 with the definition of a function that moves a DATE object from today to tomorrow. However, C++ objects do not occur individually but each one belongs to a particular class. All objects from the same class share the code which defines their functionality so that a C++ class provides a blue-print

4

for generating a whole set of objects all with the same basic characteristics. Thus a DATE class could provide enough DATE objects to fill in the entire calendar! The individual objects are distinguished from each other by their own personal data structures — this data is not shared by other objects of the class. Hence, an object in C++ is associated with:

1. Personal data
2. Code shared with other objects of the class

These two elements should be viewed as internal to the object so that the implementation details are hidden from the outside world — this notion is known as 'encapsulation'. Of course, a program must be able to send requests to an object (such as setting the Day, Month and Year fields of a DATE object or asking it to move on a day) and the object may want to acknowledge these requests. The solution is to provide a well-defined communications interface for passing messages to and from the object. As long as the program makes requests through the interface and leaves the internal processing to the object, encapsulation is guaranteed. In C++ an interface is implemented as a series of functions and requests are sent to an object by invoking the appropriate functions. The details are covered in chapters 5 and 6 but the following figure demonstrates the essential ideas:

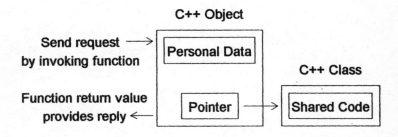

The benefit of encapsulating object implementation details and instead communicating through an interface is that code is modularised and interdependencies are reduced. Indeed one object may be substituted for another as long as they both support the same interface — this is the concept of 'polymorphism' and it is discussed more fully in chapters 13 and 14.

1.3 Building a C++ Program

The construction of a C++ program can be quite a complicated business so it is important to understand the three main steps involved. Each of these steps uses a different tool:

1. Editor
2. Compiler
3. Linker

The editor is used to produce the text files containing the C++ source code. These files are fed to the compiler which checks them for errors in syntax and (assuming all is well) proceeds to convert them into object files — these contain a machine language version of the code. Finally, the linker combines all the object files into a single executable file. The process is illustrated in the following figure:

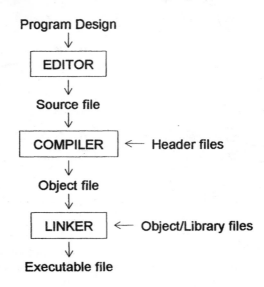

Program Design
↓
EDITOR
↓
Source file
↓
COMPILER ← Header files
↓
Object file
↓
LINKER ← Object/Library files
↓
Executable file

The figure shows that there are many different types of files. To help distinguish between the various types, each filename usually ends with the following extensions:

source file: `.cpp` or `.cxx`
header file: `.h`
object file: `.o` or `.obj`
library file: `.lib`
executable file: `.exe`

The source files contain C++ code consisting predominantly of statements for data storage allocation and data processing. The C++ program statements which specify data structures and function parameter formats typically appear in the header files. Header files are also a good place for constant definition statements. Each header file may be shared by a number of different source files all of which use the data structures, constants and functions declared in the header. A source file should contain include directives for the compiler that name the header files required:

```
#include <system.h>
#include "user.h"
```

There are two flavours of include directive — for header files supplied by the system the filename must be enclosed by angle brackets < > whilst for user-defined headers double quotes " " are required instead. The include directives typically appear at the head of a source file so that the included specification statements and constant definitions are placed before any other statements.

The code which implements the functions declared in the header files is provided by separately compiled object files and is linked into the executable file by the linker. A collection of related object files may be packaged into a single library file. This simplifies the process of providing the linker with all the necessary object files (of which there may be many).

7

1.4 The Hello Program

It is time to try your hand at producing a C++ program. Every C++ program must contain the definition of a function called `main()` which performs all the processing for the program. When a C++ program is run control passes to the `main()` function and after the `main()` function returns the program execution ceases. The value returned from the `main()` function may be used by the operating system as the exit code for the program — a value of zero typically indicates that processing completed normally. In a Windows based environment the `main()` function is replaced by the `WinMain()` function but the overall process is basically unchanged. The program shown below prints `Hello!` on the screen:

```
#include <iostream.h>
int main(void) {
    cout << "Hello!\n";
    return 0;
}
```

This is a small program but there are lots of things to understand. Firstly, the format of the `main()` function is specified by the C++ language itself — it takes no parameters (indicated by the keyword **void**) and returns an integer result. In this case, the **return** statement passes a zero value back to the operating system. The only program statement to perform any useful processing is:

```
cout << "Hello!\n";
```

The `Hello!` message is provided as a character string value which must be enclosed in double quotes. The output operator `<<` prints this string on the screen by sending it to the output stream `cout` (console output). The output stream `cout` is in fact an object defined in the header file `iostream.h` and so this header must be included with a suitable directive to the compiler:

```
#include <iostream.h>
```

The output stream object `cout` is responsible for actually printing the `Hello!` string on the screen. Finally, the `\n` part of the character string is an escape sequence (newline) that tells the `cout` object to position the cursor at the start of the next line.

1.5 Class Libraries and Software Components

An object rarely exists in isolation and will usually be designed to work in connection with other objects. For example, in a document application one object may manage the document as a whole and act in concert with other objects, each of which controls an individual page within the document. There are essentially two ways to group objects into a larger functional unit:

1. Class Libraries
2. Software Components

A class library is simply a collection of related class definitions. It is distributed with a set of header files that describe the object interfaces provided by the library — these header files must be included within the source files of any application using the library. The other half of the distribution consists of precompiled object code that provides the implementation of the library classes — this may be linked to the application code during the build operation or dynamically during execution. The important point to note is that the library and application are tightly bound together and so changes to the class library nearly always require that the application executable be rebuilt. On the other hand, the objects within a software component are entirely separate from the main application code and are manipulated only through pointers to object interfaces. Consequently, the main application and any components it uses may be updated independently without continual rebuilding. The following figure shows the construction of an application from components:

Main Application
Component

Reusable Component

Object	Object
Object	

Object	Object

Each application represents an activity performed by the user such as searching a database, word-processing or sending an e-mail message. The application typically consists of several components each providing the functionality for some aspect of the application's overall processing. For example, a database application may employ one component to interact with the user and another to manipulate the database. Within each component are objects that together implement the services provided by the component. Every object is controlled by sending it messages through a communications interface — in fact, an object may support multiple interfaces, each one representing a different facet of the object's operation. Finally, the object interfaces are composed of various functions and sending a request to an object is achieved by invoking the appropriate function. Chapters 11 to 13 look at class libraries and discuss how to design classes for inclusion in a library whilst chapter 14 focuses on software components.

1.6 Software Reusability

One excellent motive for working with objects is to simplify the task of developing software which can be readily reused. Class libraries and software components permit such reuse but are essentially just ways of packaging C++ classes. However, the C++ language itself provides three basic mechanisms for enabling software reuse.

These mechanisms are:

1. Object Linking and Embedding
2. Inheritance
3. Templates

The first option simply allows one object to be incorporated within another, either directly (embedding) or through a pointer (linking). The functionality provided by the inner object is readily available to the outer object with no further coding cost. Inheritance relies on the derivation of one C++ class from another (base) class. The derived class automatically inherits many of the characteristics of the base class. The mechanism of inheritance is discussed in detail in chapter 13. Finally, templates provide a means of creating several C++ classes from the definition of a single template class thus avoiding unnecessary code duplication. C++ template classes are the subject of chapter 12.

2. Data Types and Expressions

Chapter 1 introduced the notion of C++ data types — there are both basic C++ data types defined by the language and also structured types which may be user-defined. C++ provides built-in operators to manipulate data of the basic types whilst object classes can provide similar functionality for structured data types. This chapter details the basic types provided by C++ and looks at ways in which they may be combined into structured types. Every constant and variable used by a program must be associated with some data type through the use of a declaration statement. Thereafter, the data may be processed in expression statements by applying various C++ operators to it. There are many types of expressions in C++ (arithmetic, assignment, comparison, logical and bitwise) but each is considered here in turn. The chapter concludes with an overview of the input/output mechanism provided by the standard stream objects (`cin` and `cout`).

2.1 Basic C++ Data Types

The C++ language only defines a small number of intrinsic data types:

`char` — character type
`short`, `int`, `long` — integer types
`float`, `double` — floating-point types

The keywords (`char`, `int`, `float`, etc.) are reserved by the C++ language and may not be used as names of user-defined types, variables, functions and so on — this is also true of other keywords (such as `struct`, `if`, `return`, etc.) which will subsequently be introduced. Anyway, a character variable is used to hold a single text character (letter `a-z` or `A-Z`, digit `0-9`, punctuation mark, space, etc.) and a character value is denoted by enclosing the character within single quotes ` ' ' `. For example:

```
char letter = 'a';
```

A collection of characters forms a string and a character string value is written within double quotes " ". The program in chapter 1 used the character string "Hello!\n" which includes the escape sequence \n (newline) — all escape sequences start with a backslash \ and they are each used to represent a single character that cannot be typed directly such as newline (\n), tab (\t) or formfeed (\f). Character strings are closely related to arrays and these are discussed in the next chapter.

An integer variable may be of type short, int or long and holds a whole number such as -1000, 0 or 33. Both positive and negative values are possible but the biggest (most positive or most negative) values that the variable can hold are implementation dependent. The principal guarantee is that the range of the allowable values increases (or remains the same) from short to int to long. An int variable should use the native integer size of the host computer which is typically 32 bits nowadays. Unsigned integer types are available by employing the keyword unsigned as follows:

```
unsigned int count;
```

The count variable then holds only positive values (or zero).

Finally, variables of type float and double hold the values of real numbers such as 3.14, 0.001 or 25E+25 which may include a fractional part. The letter E (or e) is used to express floating-point numbers in scientific notation — floating-point values are assumed to be of type double unless the letter F (or f) is appended. As with integer types the exact range of values which can be held by a float or double variable depends on the C++ implementation. Generally speaking, the float type should be used unless the double type is required for extra range or precision.

Sometimes it may be necessary to convert from one type to another — this may be achieved by employing a cast as in the following example:

```
int count;
float average = 2.5;
count = (int)average;
```

The value of the `float` expression is converted (cast) to an integer type by discarding the fractional part. The cast ensures that the compiler does not object to the assignment statement — if the conversion were made automatically (without the cast) important information may be lost. An alternative notation is:

```
count = int(average);
```

Similar conversions between other types are possible by specifying the appropriate data type in the cast statement.

There have already been several examples of a variable declaration statement. This consists of a type name followed by a variable name. Sufficient storage space is allocated to the variable to hold a value of the specified type. A slight variation of the declaration statement includes an equals sign followed by a value. In this case, the variable is initialized to hold the given value. For example:

```
int count = 10;
```

This allocates storage for the `count` variable and initializes it with the value 10. An alternative notation is:

```
int count(10);
```

If a variable holds a constant value it should be declared using the `const` keyword and an initialization value must be supplied:

```
const int TEN = 10;
```

Finally, several variables of the same type may be declared

in a single statement by using commas to separate the individual variable names:

```
int count, sum, total;
```

2.2 Structured Data Types

Now that the basic C++ types have been discussed, this section looks at combining these elements to form user-defined structured data types. Such a type is declared using the keyword `struct`. For example:

```
struct DATE {
    int Day;
    int Month;
    int Year;
};
```

The word following the `struct` keyword is the name of the new data type, here `DATE`. The specification of the structured data type is enclosed in a matched pair of braces `{ }` and a semi-colon must follow. The `DATE` type contains three elements (called fields) with the names `Day`, `Month` and `Year`. An uninitialized variable of the new type is declared as follows:

```
DATE yesterday;
```

Alternatively the variable may be assigned an initial value:

```
DATE yesterday = {1,1,1970};
```

The bracketed values in the initializer are stored in the fields of the `yesterday` variable with the first one being assigned to the `Day` field, the second to the `Month` field and the third to the `Year` field. Hence the `yesterday` variable represents 1st January 1970. As with variables of basic types, the `const` keyword may be employed to prevent a variable of a structured data type from changing its value after it has been initialized in a declaration statement:

```
const DATE yesterday = {1,1,1970};
```

An alternative way to set the individual fields of a structured data object is to use the dot operator:

```
DATE yesterday;
yesterday.Day = 1;
yesterday.Month = 1;
yesterday.Year = 1970;
```

These ideas will be developed further in chapter 6 when structured data types are extended to act as C++ objects.

Another C++ keyword related to **struct** is **union**. This is used to define a new data type as follows:

```
union RATE {
   int Percentage;
   float Fraction;
};
```

A variable of type RATE may hold either an **int** value or a **float** value but not both simultaneously since the storage space for the two fields is shared. For example:

```
RATE multiplier;
```

Here the multiplier variable may be used to hold a percentage integer value:

```
multiplier.Percentage = 75;
```

Alternatively it can hold a fractional floating-point value:

```
multiplier.Fraction = 0.75;
```

Unions are not particularly useful in C++ and will not be discussed further.

2.3 Expressions

Most data processing in C++ is performed using expressions. An expression is formed by combining constants, variables and objects with various operators. One expression can be combined within another as a sub-expression and parentheses ( ) may be used to ensure the correct order of evaluation. For example:

```
answer = 7*(3+6);
```

Every C++ expression has an effect and a result. The result is simply the value produced by the expression whilst the effect is something that happens because the expression is calculated. Many expressions have no noticeable effect — however, those that do include the assignment expressions, expressions involving the increment/decrement operators (++ and --) and expressions which invoke functions.

2.4 Arithmetic Expressions

Arithmetic operators are defined for the integer and floating-point types. There are unary operators which act on a single operand and binary operators which combine a pair of operands. The binary operators are + (add), − (subtract), * (multiply) and / (divide). For example:

```
six = 6;
seven = 7;
answer = six*seven;
```

Here the answer 42 is generated. For integers there is also the % operator which gives the remainder after dividing one integer by another:

```
int remainder = 15 % 6;
```

This initializes the remainder variable with the value 3. The unary minus operator negates a value:

```
five = 5;
answer = -five;
```

The most interesting arithmetic operators are the unary operators ++ (increment) and -- (decrement) which respectively increase or decrease the value of an integer variable by 1.

For example:

```
count = 3;
count++;
```

The second statement increments the value of `count` to 4. As well as this effect of altering the value of a variable, the increment/decrement operators also produce an expression result which may be used within a larger expression. The result of the increment/decrement sub-expression is the value of the variable either before or after it is modified (depending on whether the operator is placed to the right or left of the variable name). For example:

```
count = 3;
answer = 5 * count++;
```

The processing steps performed by the second statement are as follows:

1. The `count++` expression yields the result 3

2. Since the `++` operator follows its `count` operand, the variable's value is incremented to 4 only after the result of the sub-expression is generated

3. 5 is multiplied by 3 to give the answer 15

By contrast, the following statements use the prefix form of the operator:

```
count = 3;
answer = 5 * ++count;
```

Again the value of `count` is set to 4 but now the value of `answer` is 20.

2.5 Assignment Expressions

The `++` and `--` operators provide expressions with an effect and a result. The various assignment operators (=, +=, *= and so on) also do this. The basic assignment operator = simply assigns a value to a variable — this is the effect of the assignment expression. However, the assignment expression also produces a result which is a reference to the variable appearing on the left-hand side of the equals sign. The most common use is to chain together assignments which are then executed from right to left. For example:

```
int row, column;
row = column = 0;
```

The chained assignment expression performs the following processing:

1. The value of zero is assigned to the `column` variable

2. The sub-expression `column = 0` yields a reference to the `column` variable

3. The other assignment is then effectively `row = column` and so the value of `column` (0) is copied to `row`

The overall effect is that both `row` and `column` variables are assigned the value 0.

The other types of assignment operator combine the basic assignment operation with an arithmetic (or bitwise) operation. For example:

```
total += count;
```

This expression adds the value of `count` to the current value of `total` and then stores the result in the `total` variable as its new value. Similar operators are the `-=`, `*=`, and `/=` operators.

2.6 Comparison Expressions

Comparison expressions test a pair of operands for equality or inequality or relative ordering (less than, greater than, etc.) by using the following operators:

== equal to	!= not equal to
< less than	<= less than or equal to
> greater than	>= greater than or equal to

Do not confuse the assignment operator (=) with the equality operator (==). A comparison expression yields the logical result true (represented by a non-zero value) if the relation it represents holds, and yields false (represented by a zero value) otherwise. Some examples are shown below — note that the results of these expressions are not used here.

```
six = 6;
seven = 7;
six == seven;  (false)
six != seven;  (true)
six < seven;   (true)
six >= seven;  (false)
```

The logical result of a comparison expression may be further combined in a logical expression as discussed in the next section. Both comparison and logical expressions are typically employed to control program flow — chapter 4 discusses flow control and the associated C++ programming constructs.

2.7 Logical Expressions

Logical expressions process true (non-zero) and false (zero) values. The logical operators are:

&& and
|| or
! not

The && and || operators are binary and so take two operands. The && (and) operator yields true if both the first and the second operands are true, and yields false otherwise. On the other hand, the || (or) operator yields true if either the first or the second operand is true, and yields false otherwise. Both operators are short-circuit operators which means that the left-hand operand is always evaluated but the right-hand operand is evaluated only if the evaluation is necessary to determine the overall result of the logical expression.

Hence for the && (and) operator the procedure is:

1. Evaluate the left-hand operand
2. If it is false, return the result of the expression as false
3. Otherwise evaluate the right-hand operand
4. Return the result of the expression

The procedure for the || (or) operator is similar. For example:

```
five = 5;
six = 6;
seven = 7;
(five < six) && (six <= seven);
```

The logical && expression evaluates both of its operands and generates the result true (which is simply discarded in this example). The ! (not) operator changes true to false and false to true. Hence the following logical expression is true:

```
black = 0;
white = 1;
!(black == white);
```

Finally, the ternary operator ?: takes a logical expression as its first operand and depending whether this is true or false the operator proceeds to evaluate either its second or third operand (but not both) with the result being available for use in any containing expression.

```
six = 6;
seven = 7;
smaller = (six < seven) ? six : seven;
```

Here the variable six is tested against the variable seven and since six holds a smaller value than seven, the variable smaller is assigned the value 6.

2.8 Bitwise Expressions

The bitwise operators & (and) and | (or) combine integer values one bit at a time. For each bit position the result is defined by the following tables:

   & (and) operator | (or) operator

&	0	1
0	0	0
1	0	1

|	0	1
0	0	1
1	1	1

The following code demonstrates the effect of the bitwise operators:

```
three = 3;
nine = 9;
one = three & nine;
eleven = three | nine;
```

The variables one and eleven are assigned the values 1 and 11 respectively The unary bitwise operator ~ (not) swops bits from 0 to 1 and from 1 to 0. Bitwise expressions are typically used with flag variables where each bit of an integer acts as a flag to indicate whether or not some option is enabled. For example:

```
int flags = MATH_COPROCESSOR|MEMORY_CACHE;
```

This sets the appropriate bits in the flags variable to select the desired options.

2.9 Input and Output Streams

The Hello program in chapter 1 introduced the notion of performing input/output with data streams and used the cout output stream object to display a string on the screen. There is naturally a corresponding input stream object called cin (console input) for reading data in from the keyboard. The two stream objects cin and cout work with the stream input and output operators >> and << and they can handle all the basic C++ types such as characters, strings, integers and floating-point numbers. For example:

```
int count;
cin >> count;
count++;
cout << count << '\n';
```

This code reads in a value for the `count` variable, increments the variable and then prints it out on the screen. Note that the stream expressions can be chained from left to right — here a newline character is sent to the output stream after the `count` variable is printed. The stream objects should always appear to the left of the input/output operators.

2.10 Finding the Average

The following program demonstrates some of the ideas from this chapter. It reads in a pair of integers and stores them in the variables x and y. The average is computed and the result is printed out.

```
#include <iostream.h>

int main(void) {
   int x,y;
   float average;
   cout << "Enter two integers ...\n";
   cin >> x >> y;
   average = 0.5*(x+y);
   cout << "The average is " << average;
   cout << '\n';
   return 0;
}
```

When this program is run the following text appears on the screen:

```
Enter two integers ...
3 6
The average is 4.5
```

Note that the input values (3 and 6) are automatically echoed to the screen as they are typed. The expression statement that performs the computation is:

```
average = 0.5*(x+y);
```

Multiplication by the floating-point constant 0.5 ensures that the sum x+y is converted to a floating-point value before the average is calculated — dividing by the integer 2 would perform an integer calculation with the resulting value 4. An alternate method is to use an explicit type cast:

```
average = float(x+y)/2;
```

In any binary operation involving an integer and a floating-point value, the integer is converted to a floating-point number before the two values are combined.

3. Pointers, References and Arrays

Chapter 2 introduced the notion of allocating storage space for a variable or constant by providing a declaration statement which specifies the data type. This chapter discusses in more detail how memory storage is allocated to newly declared data and describes the use of pointers to reference these storage locations. An important feature of the C++ language is that data may be manipulated indirectly through such pointers. Arithmetic operations on the pointer themselves are also possible and these operations are especially relevant when dealing with arrays. An array is a collection of several items all of the same type — the individual elements within the array are selected through the use of an integer subscript. This chapter covers both single- and multi-dimensional arrays and also looks at character arrays (strings).

3.1 Memory Storage

A variable declaration statement may be used to allocate storage space for the variable. This storage is located somewhere within the computer's memory. The memory is organised as an array of cells each containing 8 bits (1 byte) of information. Every memory cell is assigned a unique address to identify it from all the other cells — the addresses take integer values beginning with zero at the start of memory and increasing by one for each new cell. The following figure shows the layout of memory cells:

Start of Memory

Address 0	Cell
Address 1	Cell

.

.

.

Address N-1	Cell
Address N	Cell

End of Memory

3.2 Address and Indirection Operators

A **char** variable requires only 8 bits of storage and so it is allocated a single memory cell. To find the memory address of the **char** variable, the address operator & is applied:

```
char letter;
char* cell;
cell = &letter;
```

Here the address of the letter variable is assigned to the cell variable. If the letter variable is stored in cell number 54178 then after the assignment, the cell variable will have this number as its value. The cell variable is declared as being of type **char*** which means that it is a pointer to a character variable — in this context the symbol * indicates a pointer type. Pointer variables are used to hold addresses of other variables — their value points to the memory location of the variable that they reference. The following figure illustrates the state of the letter and cell variables after the code fragment above has executed:

cell **variable**   letter **variable**

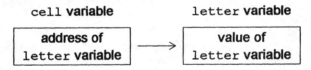

| address of | value of |
| letter variable | letter variable |

The & operator returns the address of a variable — to manipulate the variable given only its address requires the dereferencing (or indirection) operator * which converts an address into a reference to a variable. The reference can be used anywhere that the variable name could appear directly. For example, the following code prints the letter a onto the screen:

```
char letter = 'a';
cout << letter << '\n';
```

The same result can be achieved indirectly using a pointer

as follows:

```
char letter = 'a';
char* pointer = &letter;
cout << *pointer << '\n';
```

Note that a variable reference is not the same thing as the value of the variable. The following code demonstrates that a reference may appear on the left-hand side of an assignment operator (just like the variable name could) — this is not possible with a value.

```
char letter;
char* pointer = &letter;
*pointer = 'a';
cout << letter << '\n';
```

Here the `letter` variable is assigned a value indirectly using a dereferenced pointer. The final statement demonstrates this by printing out the `letter` variable directly.

3.3 References

Unlike its parent language C, C++ provides reference types in addition to its pointer types. References do not use the `&` and `*` operators but simply provide new names (aliases) for a variable. For example, here is another variant on the above theme:

```
char letter;
char& reference = letter;
reference = 'a';
cout << letter << '\n';
```

In the same way that the `*` symbol is used to declare a variable of a pointer type, the `&` symbol indicates a reference type. A reference must be initialized when it is declared and cannot be redefined to reference a new variable. References are particularly useful as function parameters and will be discussed further in chapter 5.

3.4 Pointer Types

A `char` variable can be stored in a single memory cell, but this is not generally true for variables of other types. For example, an `int` variable typically requires 32 bits of storage nowadays so each integer must occupy four memory cells. The four cells allocated are located at consecutive addresses but the exact way that the integer is stored within these cells is machine dependent. However, the `&` operator always returns the address of the first cell used. In other respects the `&` and `*` operators work with other data types in much the same way as with character variables and pointers. For example:

```
int total;
int* pointer = &total;
*pointer = 6;
cout << total << '\n';
```

Here `total` is assigned a value 6 before being printed.

A pointer which is currently pointing to no variable may be assigned the value zero (0) — this makes it a null pointer. It is then illegal to apply the indirection operator `*` to the pointer and a run-time error will result if this is attempted.

```
int* pointer = 0;
*pointer = 6; // run-time error
```

In complete contrast to null pointers C++ also supports `void` pointers. Such a pointer may reference any type of variable but cannot be dereferenced directly. To manipulate the variable the pointer must be cast to a pointer of the correct type. For example:

```
int total;
void* void_pointer = &total;
int* int_pointer = (int*)void_pointer;
*void_pointer = 6; // compile-time error
*int_pointer = 6; // okay
```

The syntax for a pointer cast is similar to a cast between basic C++ types but (as in a declaration statement) the symbol * must appear to denote a pointer type. However, the pointer type in a cast expression must be enclosed by parentheses. Any pointer type can be cast to any other (although this may not always be sensible). Some pointer casts are implicit, for example:

```
int total;
void* pointer = &total;
```

Here an implicit cast is performed from `int*` pointer type to `void*` pointer type. The explicit version is:

```
void* pointer = (void*)&total;
```

Finally, the `const` keyword may appear in a pointer declaration statement to modify the pointer type. There are two variants:

1. The pointer value must be constant
2. The value of the variable pointed at must be constant

In the first case the pointer must be initialized when it is declared and cannot subsequently be changed. Nonetheless the referenced variable may be altered indirectly through the pointer.

```
int count;
int* const pointer = &count;
*pointer = 6; // okay
```

In the second case the pointer value may change as required but the dereferenced pointer may not appear on the left-hand side of an assignment expression.

```
const int count = 9;
const int* pointer;
pointer = &count;
*pointer = 6; // compile-time error
```

Of course, the two variants can be combined and then

neither the pointer nor the variable may be modified. For example:

```
const int count = 9;
const int* const pointer = &count;
```

The `const` keyword is used in a similar fashion with references.

3.5 Pointer Arithmetic

Some arithmetic operations may be performed on the pointers themselves. The increment/decrement operators (++ and --) can be applied to a pointer just as they can to an integer variable — the only difference here is the size of the increment or decrement. With integers the value always changes by 1, but for pointers the value changes by the number of memory cells needed to store a variable of the data type associated with the pointer. For example, if an `int` variable occupies four bytes of storage then the ++ operator will increase the value of an `int*` pointer by 4 and the -- operator will decrease its value by 4. Similary, an integer value may be added to (or subtracted from) a pointer and the result is identical to applying the increment (or decrement) operator the number of times indicated by the integer value. This movement of a pointer in variable-sized steps is useful if several variables of the same type are located one after another in memory — the following section on arrays discusses this idea more fully. Finally, if two pointers are initially equal and one is moved a certain number of steps, then applying the difference operator to the two pointers yields the number of steps moved. For example:

```
pointer1 = pointer2;
pointer2++;
pointer2++;
int count = pointer2-pointer1;
```

Here the value of count is set to 2.

3.6 Arrays

Chapter 2 described how the `struct` keyword can be used to combine basic data types to form a larger structure. Another possibility is to define an array of elements all of the same basic type — the individual elements are stored one after another in memory. The C++ language provides built-in support for arrays by allowing array variables to be declared and by supplying the subscript operator `[]` to reference the elements of an array. The following statement allocates storage for an array of five integers:

```
int x[5];
```

The individual elements may be referred to as to `x[0]`, `x[1]`, ... , `x[4]` and they are stored in memory as follows:

Name	x[0]	x[1]	x[2]	x[3]	x[4]
	integer	integer	integer	integer	integer
Address	N	N+Size	N+2*Size	N+3*Size	N+4*Size

The number of memory cells used to store each integer is denoted in the figure by the quantity Size. The `sizeof` operator will indicate the number of bytes needed to store a variable of a particular type — for 32 bit integers `sizeof(int)` equals 4.

The `[]` operator is closely related to the `*` dereferencing operator and provides a reference to an element of the array. The particular element referenced is identified by the subscript which appears between the square brackets — the first element always has the subscript 0. Indeed for any subscript `n` the following identity holds:

$$x[n] \ == \ *(x+n)$$

The array name `x` on its own supplies a pointer to the first element in the array and so `x+n` is a pointer to the element with subscript `n`. Further `*(x+n)` is a reference to this element — however, the notation x[n] is usually preferred. The following code uses an initializer list to set the array elements and then sums the individual values:

```
int x[5] = {7,8,6,9,5};
int total = x[0]+x[1]+x[2]+x[3]+x[4];
```

A much better way to process arrays is to apply the looping constructs discussed in chapter 4.

3.7 Strings

Character arrays are known as strings — the C++ language allows constant string values to be defined by enclosing the characters in double quotes. The effect of such a definition is to store the array of characters somewhere in memory and to supply a character pointer that points to the first element of the array. In addition to the characters which appear between the quotes another element is automatically placed at the end of the array. This final element has the value zero and can be used to identify the end of the string. For example:

```
char* string = "Hello";
```

This statements results in the following memory usage:

string variable

The pointer must not be used to modify the elements of the string constant. If a string needs to be altered then it should be stored in a character array:

```
char string[6] = {'H','e','l','l','o',0};
```

To simplify the initialization of such arrays C++ supports the following short-hand notation:

```
char string[6] = "Hello";
```

Note that the length of the array must allow for the

terminating zero character. The elements of a character array may change as required.

Here is a short program to print out a `Help!` message. It demonstrates some of the ideas about pointers and arrays presented in this chapter.

```cpp
#include <iostream.h>

int main(void) {
  char string[6] = "Hello";
  char* letter = string;
  letter += 3;
  *letter = 'p';
  string[4] = '!';
  cout << string << '\n';
  return 0;
}
```

3.8 Multi-Dimensional Arrays

The C++ language also supports multi-dimensional arrays — these use several subscripts to identify an element within the array. For example, a checker board may be represented as a two-dimensional array with one subscript for the row and another for the column. The declaration of a multi-dimensional array is quite straightforward:

```cpp
int board[8][8];
```

The top left-hand square of the board would correspond to the element `board[0][0]` whilst for the bottom right-hand square the corresponding element would be `board[7][7]`. A general square located by the values of `row` and `column` corresponds to the array element `board[row][column]`. The elements for the `board` array are stored one after another in memory — the elements for the first row (`board[0][0]`, ... , `board[0][7]`) are stored first, followed immediately by those for the second row and so on.

4. Statements

The C++ language provides only a few program statement types and related keywords. However, nesting of statements one within another is permitted so that the basic elements can be combined to implement quite complex algorithms. This chapter summarizes the various statement types (simple, block and structured) which are available in C++. Block statements allow a number of related statements to be grouped as one — it is important to understand the interaction of block statements and data storage allocation in C++. Program execution usually flows from one statement to the next in top to bottom fashion — structured statements are designed specifically to modify this pattern of execution. The structured statements available in C++ include the conditional `if`, `if-else` and `switch` statements as well as the looping `while`, `do-while` and `for` statements.

4.1 C++ Statement Types

A C++ program consists of collection of program statements ordered from top to bottom. Some statements specify new data types or the format of function parameter lists — such statements are discussed further in chapters 5 and 6. The remaining statements implement the program's functionality by declaring variables and performing data processing — there are essentially three sorts of these statements:

1. Simple statements
2. Block statements
3. Structured statements

Examples of simple and block statements have appeared in previous chapters — this chapter is principally concerned with introducing the structured statements. The following sections each describe a different statement type.

37

4.2 Simple Statements

Simple statements are always terminated by a semi-colon (;) and come in three flavours:

1. Declaration statements
2. Expression statements
3. Transfer statements

Declaration and expression statements were discussed at length in chapters 2 and 3. Examples are:

```
int x,y;
float average;
average = float(x+y)/2;
```

Program execution usually flows from one statement to the next but this natural flow may be broken and control transferred elsewhere by the occurrence of a transfer statement. The `return` statement is one example:

```
int main(void) {
    .
    .
    .
    return 0;
}
```

Here control passes back to the operating system — chapter 5 looks at the `return` statement in more detail. Other transfer statements include:

```
break;
continue;
```

These are used in conjunction with the structured statements presented in sections 4.4 and 4.5.

4.3 Block Statements

A block statement is simply a collection of other statements bracketed by a matching pair of braces { } and serves to group the enclosed statements as a single statement. Note that no semi-colon appears at the end of a

block statement:

{ Statement Statement ... Statement Statement }

A block statement is employed where the syntax of C++ permits only one statement but several statements are required to perform the necessary processing. Of course, the enclosed statements can themselves be block statements and so blocks can be nested to any depth.

One important point about block statements is that they influence the allocation of data storage space in memory. A declaration statement is used to allocate the storage space initially. If the declaration statement is not enclosed by a block statement then a global variable is defined which exists for the entire time that the program is running. However, if the declaration statement is enclosed by a block statement then a local variable is defined. The local variable only exists until program control exits the (innermost) block statement containing the variable's declaration statement. Once a local variable ceases to exist its storage space is deallocated and any pointers which reference the variable should no longer be used. For example:

```
int x; // global variable

int main(void) {
  int y; // local variable
  {
    int z; // local variable
  }
  return 0;
}
```

The local variable `z` ceases to exist when the inner block is exited and the local variable `y` ceases to exist when the `main()` function returns.

Different variables in different blocks may have the same name. When the name is used in an expression it refers to the variable declared within the innermost block containing the expression statement.

For example:

```
#include <iostream.h>

int main(void) {
  int x = 1;
  {
    int x = 2;
    cout << "x = " << x << '\n';
  }
}
```

This program will print:

```
x = 2
```

since the name x in the stream output statement refers to the x variable declared within the inner block.

4.4 Conditional Structured Statements

Structured statements control how the thread of execution flows through a C++ program. The syntax for a structured statement is defined by the C++ language — such a statement always contains one or more other statements within itself. There are two sorts of structured statement:

1. Conditional statements
2. Looping statements

These are discussed in this section and the next respectively.

The simplest conditional statement is the **if** statement — this structured statement executes a contained statement conditionally according to the result of a logical expression.

```
if (Expression)
  Statement
```

The contained statement is executed if the bracketed expression is true (non-zero) but if the expression is false

40

(zero) then control passes directly to the statement following the `if` statement and the contained statement is not executed. For example:

```
int total = 6;
if (total<9)
  total++;
cout << total;
```

The comparision `total<9` is true so the `total` variable is incremented and the value 7 is printed.

There is also an `if-else` conditional structured statement:

```
if (Expression)
  Statement1
else
  Statement2
```

Here either Statement1 or Statement2 is executed (but not both) depending on whether the expression evaluates to true or false. The action is very similar to the `?:` operator described in chapter 2. For example:

```
if (x<0)
  absolute = -x;
else
  absolute = x;
```

or equivalently:

```
absolute = (x<0) ? -x : x;
```

Here the `absolute` variable is made to hold the magnitude of `x` by reversing the sign of negative values.

As with block statements nesting of structured statements is possible — in fact (with a few restrictions) all statement types are interchangeable as far as nesting is concerned.

An example of nested **if-else** statements follows:

```
cout << "The letter is";
if (letter == 'a')
  cout << " 'a'.";
else if (letter == 'b')
  cout << " 'b'.";
else
  cout << " not 'a' or 'b'.";
cout << '\n';
```

The C++ language provides the **switch** statement as an alternative method of coding such tests:

```
switch (Expression)
  BlockStatement
```

The above example may be recoded as:

```
cout << "The letter is";
switch (letter) {
  case 'a':
    cout << " 'a'.";
    break;
  case 'b':
    cout << " 'b'.";
    break;
  default:
    cout << " not 'a' or 'b'.";
    break;
}
cout << '\n';
```

The **case** labels specify possible values of the bracketed expression which follows the **switch** keyword. Control passes to the statement immediately after the appropriate **case** label (or after the **default** label if no other labels match). The **break** statements transfer control out of the block statement contained by the **switch** statement.

4.5 Looping Structured Statements

The second kind of structured statements are looping constructs. The simplest is the `while` statement which has the following syntax:

```
while (Expression)
    Statement
```

The processing performed by the `while` statement is depicted in the following figure.

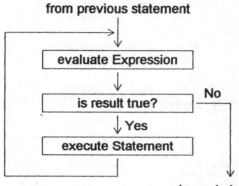

The contained statement forms the body of a loop which is repeatedly executed until the logical expression evaluates as false (zero). A typical application is to copy one character string to another:

```
char message[6];
char* string = "Hello";
int i = 0;
while (message[i] = *string) {
  i++;
  string++;
}
cout << message << '\n';
```

Here the zero value at the end of the string causes the

`while` loop to terminate. A null statement sometimes appears as the body of a `while` loop. For example, the previous loop may be rewritten as:

```
while (message[i++] = *string++)
    ;
```

The lone semi-colon marks the end of a null statement contained by the `while` statement.

The `break` and `continue` transfer statements may appear within the loop body to alter the usual program flow of the loop. The `break` statement immediately exits the loop whilst the `continue` statement ends the current iteration of the loop body and starts to re-evaluate the controlling expression.

A slight variation of the `while` statement is the `do-while` statement which always executes the loop body at least once.

```
do
    Statement
while (Expression);
```

The operation of a `do-while` loop is depicted below.

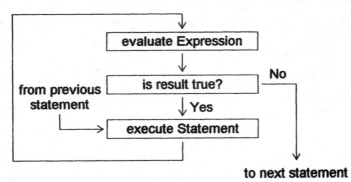

The `while` loop is typically employed when the number of iterations is unknown beforehand — alternatively if the number of iterations can be predicted a `for` loop may be more suitable.

> `for` (Initializer; ControlExpression; IterationExpression)
> Statement

The `for` statement performs the processing shown in the following figure:

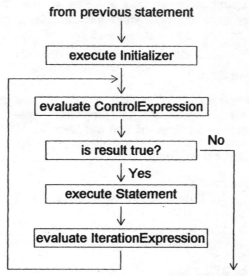

from previous statement

execute Initializer

evaluate ControlExpression

is result true? — No

↓Yes

execute Statement

evaluate IterationExpression

to next statement

In comparison to a `while` loop the main difference is that initialization may be performed and after each pass through the loop an iteration expression is evaluated — this expression typically updates the value of a loop counter. For example:

```
int x[5] = {5,7,9,8,6};
int total = 0;
for (int i=0; i<5; i++)
   total += x[i];
cout << "The total is " << total << '\n';
```

Here the five elements of the x array are summed to calculate the value of total. Note that a variable may be declared as part of the loop initialization — the variable continues to exist until the block containing the for statement is exited.

As with a while loop, the break and continue transfer statements may appear within the body of a for loop to alter the usual flow of control. The break statement immediately exits the loop whilst the continue statement transfers control to the evaluation of the iteration expression.

4.6 Insertion Sort

A simple method of sorting a list of integers is the insertion sort. The following program implements an insertion sort for an array of five integers.

```
#include <iostream.h>

int main(void) {
  cout << "Enter five integers ...\n";
  int x[5];
  int i,j,n,t;
  for (n=0; n<5; n++) {
    cin >> t;
    i = 0;
    while (i<n && t>x[i])
      i++;
    for (j=n; j>i; j--)
      x[j] = x[j-1];
    x[i] = t;
  }
  cout << "Sorted list:";
  for (n=0; n<5; n++)
    cout << ' ' << x[n];
  cout << '\n';
  return 0;
}
```

Starting with an empty array, each item in turn is inserted at the correct position within the array — any existing items at the end of the array are moved along to make room for the new item. The `while` statement:

```
while (i<n && t>x[i])
    i++;
```

finds the correct place to insert the new item and the `for` statement:

```
for (j=n; j>i; j--)
    x[j] = x[j-1];
```

moves existing items which follow the new item.

5. Functions

All data processing in a C++ program is performed by functions — the operating system passes control to the `main()` function and expression statements within `main()` invoke yet other functions. A C++ function is a block of code which accepts a number of data items as input, performs various operations using these parameters and finally yields a result. Whilst the function is executing it may also produce side-effects such as opening a file, clearing the screen or updating a database. This chapter details the process of declaring, defining and invoking a function. A function declaration specifies the function parameter list and return type — the corresponding function definition lists the processing steps which will be performed when the function is invoked. The various possibilities for function call semantics (by-value, by-pointer and by-reference) are also discussed. Finally, a function name in C++ may be overloaded by providing different function definitions for different types of parameter — optional parameters are also supported.

5.1 C++ Functions

Chapter 1 outlined the use of functions in a C++ to perform data processing — the whole of a C++ program is contained within the single function `main()`. Each C++ function is a modular piece of code which accepts a number of data parameters, performs calculations using these parameters and finally generates a result — the result can be processed further within an expression statement. There are three important steps involved in working with a C++ function:

1. Function declaration
2. Function definition
3. Function invocation

A function declaration statement specifies the format of the function parameter list and the type of result returned by the function. For example:

```
char Letter(int);
```

This statement specifies that the function `Letter()` takes a single parameter of type `int` and returns a result of type `char`. The `Letter()` function is intended to provide the letter of the alphabet corresponding to its integer parameter — for example, a parameter value of 1 returns the letter a whilst a parameter value of 26 returns the letter z. The processing performed by the `Letter()` function must be defined somewhere — the definition should follow the function declaration statement.

```
char Letter(int i) {
  char alphabet[28] =
    " abcdefghijklmnopqrstuvwxyz";
  return alphabet[i];
}
```

The processing performed by the function is defined by a series of program statements enclosed by a matching pair of braces { } — in other words a function is defined using a single block statement. The general syntax is:

ReturnType FunctionName(ParameterList)
    BlockStatement

Individual parameters within the parameter list are separated by commas. If the function requires no parameters the keyword **void** should appear between the parentheses. Similarly the keyword **void** is placed before the function name to denote that the function does not return a result.

For the `Letter()` function defined above, the result is taken from an array of characters. Note that `alphabet[0]` is the first element of this array and it contains a space character — similarly `alphabet[27]` is the final element of the array and it contains a zero character.

To invoke the `Letter()` function requires a statement such as:

```
char letter = Letter(13);
```

This assigns the value `'m'` to the `letter` variable.

Any statement which invokes a function must appear after the corresponding function declaration. However, the relative position of the function definition and the function invocation is unimportant. Indeed these may occur in different source files if these files share a header that contains the function declaration.

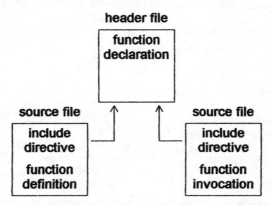

The function definition provides an implementation of the function whilst the function declaration defines a communications interface between the function and any other code which wishes to invoke it. This approach of separating implementation from interface is particularly important for objects — the next chapter discusses this idea further.

5.2 Invoking a Function

This section examines the processing which occurs when a function is invoked. For each function invocation the parameters of the function are assigned actual values (arguments). These are provided by the statement which invokes the function. For example:

```
char letter = Letter(13);
char Letter(int i) {
    .
    .
}
```

Here the argument 13 is assigned to the i parameter. The variable i is local to the block statement defining the Letter() function and ceases to exist when the function returns. In particular, if the Letter() function is invoked with a variable as an argument then i is initialized using the value of the variable but if i were to be subsequently modified these changes would not be reflected by the argument variable. For example:

```
int position = 13;
char letter = Letter(position);

char Letter(int i) {
    char alphabet[27] =
      "abcdefghijklmnopqrstuvwxyz";
    return alphabet[--i];
}
```

Here the value of the position argument is copied to i during initialization of the parameter. Then i is decremented to account for the fact that array subscripts are zero-based. However, the position variable itself is unaffected by the function call.

These semantics are known as call-by-value since only the value of the argument is passed to the function. Similarly return-by-value semantics are applied when returning the result of a function. For the Letter() function the character selected from the alphabet array is copied to a temporary character variable. The function then returns and the alphabet array ceases to exist. The value of the temporary variable is available within the statement that

52

invoked the function and so can be assigned to the `letter` variable. However, once the invoking statement finishes its processing the temporary variable disappears too.

5.3 Pointers and References

There may be times when a function must modify data that exists outside of the function. C++ provides two methods to circumvent the limitations of call-by-value semantics:

1. call-by-pointer
2. call-by-reference

The first option is simply an extension of the call-by-value approach but passes a pointer to a variable instead of the variable itself — the value of the pointer argument is still copied to the corresponding function parameter. For example:

```
int x = 3;
Square(&x);
cout << "x = " << x << '\n';

void Square(int* pointer) {
  int i = *pointer;
  *pointer = i*i;
  return;
}
```

The `Square()` function squares the value of an integer variable. The address of the variable should be passed as the argument to the function and this address is used to initialize the `pointer` parameter. By dereferencing this pointer the actual value (not a copy) of the `x` variable can be manipulated. Hence the code prints:

```
x = 9
```

Note that the `Square()` function has a **void** return type since it does not produce a result — it is invoked only for its effect.

An array is automatically passed to a function using call-by-pointer semantics — the function parameter receives a pointer to the first element of the array. For example:

```
int a[5] = {6,9,7,5,8};
int answer = Sum(a);

int Sum(int* array) {
  int total = 0;
  for (int i=0; i<5; i++)
    total += array[i];
  return total;
}
```

The second method of modifying the value of a function argument is to employ a C++ reference. The `Square()` example can be rewritten as:

```
int x = 3;
Square(x);
cout << "x = " << x << '\n';

void Square(int& i) {
  i = i*i;
  return;
}
```

The syntax is often more elegant when references are substituted for pointers since the address and dereferencing operators are unnecessary. Within the `Square()` function the reference `i` is an alias for the `x` variable and so any operations involving `i` affect `x` directly.

5.4 Return Values

As discussed in section 5.2 the value returned from a function is usually stored in a temporary variable. However, as with function parameter passing there are actually three possibilities:

1. return-by-value
2. return-by-pointer
3. return-by-reference

The first option returns a temporary value which exists only whilst the expression which invoked the function is being evaluated. The second option is a variant of the first where the temporary variable holds a pointer to more persistent data. For example:

```
char* word = "alphabet";
char letter = *Letter(word,5);
cout << "The fifth letter is: ";
cout << letter << '\n';

char* Letter(char* string,int i) {
  i--;
  return (string+i);

}
```

The Letter() function returns a pointer to the fifth letter of the "alphabet" string. The pointer is temporary but the character pointed at is more permanent. It is important to avoid mistakes such as the following:

```
char* Letter(int i) {
  char alphabet[28] =
   " abcdefghijklmnopqrstuvwxyz";
  return (alphabet+i);
}
```

Here a pointer is returned which references data that no longer exists after the function returns.

The third option for returning a result from a function is to employ a reference. Again it is important to ensure that the reference is not for a variable which is local to the function. The following example computes the fourth power of the x variable:

```
int x = 3;
Square(Square(x));
cout << "x = " << x << '\n';

int& Square(int& i) {
  i = i*i;
  return i;
}
```

This code prints:

```
x = 81
```

The inner call of Square() squares x from 3 to 9 and returns a reference to x. The outer call then uses this reference to again square x from 9 to 81.

5.5 The const Keyword

The const keyword can be employed with function declarations in many different ways. These can be categorized as follows:

1. constant parameters
2. constant result
3. constant object

The first two possibilities apply when pointers or references are used to pass function parameters or return a result. Chapter 3 discussed the basic meaning of the const keyword with pointers and references but there are two important applications relating specifically to functions. Firstly, call-by-pointer or call-by-reference semantics may be used simply to avoid the overhead involved in copying the value of an argument to the corresponding parameter. The argument is not to be modified by the function and this should be indicated by placing the const keyword in the function parameter list before the relevant parameter. For example:

```
int Weekday(const DATE&);
```

This declares the Weekday() function as accepting a reference to a variable of the user-defined type DATE — the const keyword indicates that the DATE variable will not be altered by the Weekday() function through this reference.

Similarly, return-by-pointer or return-by-reference semantics may be employed to return a result without having to copy the value to a temporary variable. However, if the variable referred to must not be modified using the returned pointer or reference then the keyword const should precede the function return type.

Finally, the third use of `const` with functions places the keyword after the function parameter list. This usage is relevant only to functions defined for a C++ class and will be covered in the next chapter — the `const` keyword indicates that invoking the function will not change the internal state of the associated object.

5.6 Function Pointers

Just as the name of an array is automatically converted to a pointer so is the name of a function when written without an argument list. Such function pointers may be used to invoke the function indirectly. For example:

```
void (*pointer)(void);

if (arriving)
  pointer = Hello;
else
  pointer = Goodbye;
(*pointer)();

void Hello(void) {
  cout << "Hello!\n";
}

void Goodbye(void) {
  cout << "Goodbye!\n";
}
```

The declaration statement:

```
void (*pointer)(void);
```

declares the `pointer` variable as being a pointer to a function taking no arguments and returning no result. Depending on the logical value of `arriving` the pointer is set to reference either the `Hello()` function or the `Goodbye()` function. The expression:

```
(*pointer)();
```

invokes the function referenced by the pointer and so prints either `Hello!` or `Goodbye!` as appropriate.

57

5.7 Function Overloading

A feature of C++ is the ability to define several functions all with the same name but having different types of parameters — this is known as "function overloading". The particular function invoked is determined by the types of arguments passed to the function. The actual selection procedure is quite involved but overloaded functions are generally easy to use. For example:

```
char* Next(char*);
char* Next(char*,int);
```

The Next() functions are used to move a pointer along a string — the first function always moves the pointer one step whilst the second function allows the number of steps to be specified by an integer parameter. Typical implementations might be:

```
char* Next(char* string) {
  return ++string;
}

char* Next(char* string,int i) {
  return (string+i);
}
```

An alternative approach here would be to declare a single Next() function with an optional parameter:

```
char * Next(char*,int = 1);

char* Next(char* string,int i) {
  return (string+i);
}
```

The integer parameter defaults to the value 1 if it is not supplied in the argument list. Optional parameters must always be located at the end of the parameter list.

Only the function name and the parameter types are used to distinguish one overloaded function from another. Consequently there cannot be two functions which differ only in their return type.

6. Classes and Objects

C++ classes form the basis for all object oriented mechanisms supported by the language. A C++ class can be obtained by combining a user-defined data structure with functions designed to manipulate this data. The technique permits a C++ class to provide its objects with similar facilities to those supplied intrinsically by C++ for built-in data types. A class specification lists both object data structures and related function declarations — these class functions are defined in a similar manner to the global functions discussed in Chapter 5. Objects of a C++ class are created in essentially the same way as variables of basic and structured data types although the procedure is slightly more complicated. Thereafter the program code sends requests to an object by invoking the appropriate functions and the object manages its own internal data structures — a reply may be returned as the result of the function invocation. The `.` and `->` operators are used to associate a function call with a particular object. The object implementation details are hidden from the outside world and all communications pass through an interface specified by the format declarations for the class functions.

6.1 From `struct` to `class`

Chapter 2 discussed the use of the `struct` keyword for specifying structured data types. This section details the extension of a structured data type into a C++ class by the addition of functions which will manipulate the data. Here the starting point is the structured data type DATE:

```
struct DATE {
   int Day;
   int Month;
   int Year;
};
```

The first step is to change the keyword `struct` to `class` and add some function declarations.

For example:

```
class DATE {
public:
  void SetDate(int,int,int);
  int GetDay(void) const;
  int GetMonth(void) const;
  int GetYear(void) const;
  int Day;
  int Month;
  int Year;
};
```

The SetDate() function takes three integer parameters which will be assigned to the Day, Month and Year fields. The GetDay(), GetMonth() and GetYear() functions each return the value of an individual field — the const keywords following each function indicate that the functions do not alter the internal state of the DATE object. The public keyword is explained in section 6.3. The next step is to provide function definitions:

```
void DATE::SetDate(int day,int month,int year){
  Day = day;
  Month = month;
  Year = year;
}

int DATE::GetDay(void) const {
  return Day;
}

int DATE::GetMonth(void) const {
  return Month;
}

int DATE::GetYear(void) const {
  return Year;
}
```

The class name DATE followed by the :: operator must precede the function name in each of the definitions. Within these functions the `Day`, `Month` and `Year` fields are simply referred to by name.

6.2 C++ Objects

Now that the `DATE` class has been defined it is possible to create objects of the class. The notation is identical to that for variables of basic or structured data types:

```
DATE yesterday;
```

The declaration statement allocates storage space for the `yesterday` object — the object ceases to exist when the block containing this declaration is exited. The object contains its own personal `Day`, `Month` and `Year` fields as well as a pointer to the functions which it shares with all other objects of the `DATE` class. As with a variable of a structured data type, the fields contained by an object may be referenced by applying the . operator:

```
yesterday.Day = 1;
yesterday.Month = 1;
yesterday.Year = 1970;
```

However, the object's functions may be invoked in a similar manner. For example:

```
yesterday.SetDate(1,1,1970);
int month = yesterday.GetMonth();
```

An alternative way to describe the action of each of these statements is to say that the `yesterday` object receives a message, performs some internal processing and sends back a reply if appropriate.

6.3 Encapsulation

The technique of communicating with an object using messages allows the functionality of the object to be split into two:

1. Interface
2. Implementation

The communications interface fixes the format of messages

61

sent and received by the object — it is specified by the function declaration statements for the object's class. Upon receipt of a message, the object performs some internal processing — the implementation details are determined by the data structures which the object contains and by the related function definitions. The important point is that when the implementation is isolated from the interface then the internal workings of the object may be hidden from the outside world — this idea is known as 'encapsulation' and it is depicted in the following figure:

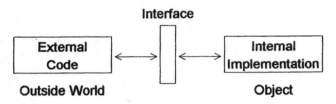

External code can continue to successfully communicate through the interface even if the implementation is changed. For example, the implementation of the DATE class may be hidden by addition of the **private** keyword:

```
class DATE {
public:
   void SetDate(int,int,int);
   int GetDay(void) const;
   int GetMonth(void) const;
   int GetYear(void) const;
private:
   int Day;
   int Month;
   int Year;
};
```

The **public** keyword allows the fields and functions which follow to be referenced by any program code. However, the **private** keyword restricts this activity just to code within the function definitions for the class. Since C++ objects share function code this means that encapsulation occurs at the class level — C++ is thus class oriented rather than object oriented and this fact is exploited in later chapters. Anyway, the `Day`, `Month` and `Year` fields are now private to the `DATE` class and implementation details are consequently hidden. The class can change its implementation but retain the same interface:

```
class DATE {
public:
  void SetDate(int,int,int);
  int GetDay(void) const;
  int GetMonth(void) const;
  int GetYear(void) const;
private:
  int Seconds;
};
```

Here the date is stored internally as the number of seconds since 1st January 1970. Existing external code will still function as before but needs to be recompiled with the new class specification. Chapters 13 and 14 look at ways in which even this recompilation step can be avoided.

6.4 Object Pointers

Pointers (and references) can be used with objects in much the same way as with variables. The `&` operator gives the address of an object and the `*` operator dereferences an object pointer.

```
DATE yesterday;
DATE* pointer = &yesterday;
```

The `.` operator will work with a dereferenced object pointer to reference a field or function:

```
(*pointer).Year = 1970;
(*pointer).SetDate(1,1,1970);
```

However, it is more usual to apply the `->` operator directly

63

to the pointer:

```
pointer->Year = 1970;
pointer->SetDate(1,1,1970);
```

Finally, within the function definitions for a class the keyword **this** supplies a pointer to the object for which the function was invoked. The **this** pointer is used implicitly within these functions to reference the object's fields and functions. For example, the SetDate() function definition appearing in section 6.1 may be rewritten in explicit form as follows:

```
void DATE::SetDate(int day, int month, int year) {
    this->Day = day;
    this->Month = month;
    this->Year = year;
}
```

One possible use for the **this** keyword is to return a reference to the object itself:

```
DATE& DATE::GetDate(void) {
        .
        .
    return *this;
}
```

6.5 Data and Function Categories

Data which is declared in a statement that does not lie within a block is global data — it is initialized before the main() function starts to run and continues to exist until the program terminates. Similarly, a function which is declared outside of a class specification is a global function and it can be invoked from anywhere within the program. The names of global data and functions can be hidden by the same name being declared within a block or class but the global version is always available by prefixing the name with the :: operator.

For example:

```
int x = 1;

int main(void) {
  int x = 2;
  cout << "x = " << ::x << '\n';
  return 0;
}
```

This will print:

```
x = 1
```

since ::x refers to the global variable x.

Global functions generally cannot manipulate data or invoke functions which are private elements of a class. However, a function can be granted this right by including it in the class specification preceded by the **friend** keyword. For example:

```
class DATE;
void Print(DATE&);

class DATE {
  friend void Print(DATE&);
private:
  int Day;
  int Month;
  int Year;
};

void Print(DATE& date) {
  cout << "The date is ";
  cout << date.Day << '/';
  cout << date.Month << '/';
  cout << date.Year << '.';
  cout << '\n';
}
```

The forward declaration:

```
class DATE;
```

allows the `Print()` function to use the `DATE&` type in its declaration statement. The `Print()` function prints out a representation of the `DATE` object — chapter 9 demonstrates a more elegant way to do this. The **friend** keyword can also be used with functions belonging to another class — alternatively all functions of another class may be made into friend functions by a single statement such as:

```
friend class ClassName;
```

within the specification of the first class.

Finally, the keyword **static** may appear in a class specification to denote that a field or function belongs to the class as a whole rather than to individual objects of the class. Such elements may be referenced by prefixing their names with the class name and the `::` operator. For example:

```
class MATH {
public:
  const static float Pi;
  static int Random(void);
};

const float MATH::Pi = 3.142;

int Main(void) {
  cout << "The random number is: ";
  cout << MATH::Random() << '\n';
  return 0;
}
```

Static data fields should be declared globally — constant fields like `Pi` must also be initialized. A good place for these declarations is in the class source file along with the function definitions — if they appear in a header file there is the possibility of allocating storage for the same data more than once. The `Random()` function returns a random number and can be invoked without first creating any objects of type MATH.

6.6 Creating and Destroying Objects

There are essentially four categories of objects:

1. Temporary objects
2. Local objects
3. Dynamic objects
4. Global objects

These are listed in order of generally increasing length of existence. Temporary objects exist only within the statement which processes them — they are usually created implicitly as function return values but the next chapter discusses how to create temporary objects explicitly. Local objects exist from the point at which their declaration statement is encountered until the block containing this statement is exited. Dynamic objects are created and destroyed explicitly by the programmer with the `new` and `delete` keywords — this is the topic of chapter 10. Finally, global objects exist throughout the execution of the program. The following chapter examines the object creation and destruction processes in more detail.

7. Constructors and Destructors

During the execution of a program numerous C++ objects may be created and destroyed. When an object is created storage space is allocated for it in memory — deallocation of the storage occurs when the object is destroyed. At creation the object may require initialization to place it in a well-defined state and to acquire any system resources that it utilizes — similarly during finalization the object may need to release any resources it holds before ceasing to exist. To define the initialization and finalization procedures for an object its class must provide constructor and destructor functions that are implicitly invoked to perform the necessary processing. The constructor function can be overloaded to provide a variety of ways of initializing an object. A constructor which takes no parameters acts as a default constructor — it is invoked when no initialization arguments are available. Finally, a temporary object may be created by an explicit call to a class constructor. These objects can serve as constant values within expressions in a similar fashion to the integer, floating-point and character values supported directly by the C++ language.

7.1 Object Creation and Destruction

Most objects are created when a declaration for the object is encountered — the object continues to exist until the block containing the declaration statement is exited. Two operations occur when an object is created:

1. Storage Allocation
2. Object Initialization

and similarly two operations occur when the object is destroyed:

1. Object Finalization
2. Storage Deallocation

The storage allocation and deallocation operations are fairly straightforward — sufficient memory space is made available to the object to hold its data and so on. Chapter 10 delves a little more deeply into the management of memory storage. The initialization operation puts the object into a well-defined state and acquires any system resources that the object may need to perform its function — the corresponding finalization operation releases these resources. Unless explicitly specified by the program code both initialization and finalization operations are effectively null.

7.2 Constructors and Destructors

To provide initialization and finalization for an object its class must define respectively constructor and destructor functions. The name of the constructor is the same as the name of the class whilst the name of destructor prepends the ~ character to the class name. For example:

test.h:

```
class TEST {
public:
   TEST(void);
   ~TEST(void);
};
```

test.cpp:

```
#include "test.h"

TEST::TEST(void) {
   cout << "Initializing ...\n";
}

TEST::~TEST(void) {
   cout << "Finalizing ...\n";
}
```

The TEST class performs no useful purpose except to demonstrate when the constructor TEST() and destructor ~TEST() are invoked. The class specification appears in the test.h header file whilst the function definitions appear in the `text.cpp` source file. Note that constructors and destructors do not have return types — furthermore a destructor always has an empty parameter list.

Here is a program to test the `TEST` class:

```
#include <iostream.h>
#include "test.h"

int main(void) {
  cout << "Before Object Creation\n";
  {
    TEST test;
    cout << "Object Exists\n";
  }
  cout << "After Object Destruction\n";
  return 0;
}
```

The `TEST` class specification within the `test.h` header file is included by the directive:

```
#include "test.h"
```

The sharing of a header file between two source files is depicted at the end of section 5.1 — the discussion there regarding global functions applies equally well to classes. The program produces the following output:

```
Before Object Creation
Initializing ...
Object Exists
Finalizing ...
After Object Destruction
```

Hence the constructor is implicitly invoked to perform initialization when the object is created by its declaration statement — the constructor call occurs immediately after memory storage has been allocated for the object. Similarly, the destructor is implicitly invoked to perform finalization just before the object's storage space is deallocated — here the object is destroyed when the inner block containing its declaration statement is exited.

7.3 The Default Constructor

A class can define only a single destructor but it may have several constructors — this is an example of the function overloading technique discussed in section 5.7. The default constructor is the constructor which takes no parameters. If no constructors are explicitly defined then the implicit null constructor acts as a default constructor. If any constructors are explicitly defined then a default constructor must be supplied if it is needed — a constructor which has all its parameters optional can serve as a default constructor. The default constructor is needed in situations where an object of the class is created but no parameters are available. For example, an object declaration statement which does not include an initializer invokes the default constructor:

```
TEST test;
```

Similarly, if an array of objects are declared then the default constructor is used to initialize each element of the array:

```
TEST test[10];
```

7.4 Constructor Overloading

As noted in the previous section, a class may overload its constructor function. The COMPLEX class will serve as an example of constructor overloading — the class is further developed in chapters 8 and 9. An object of the COMPLEX class represents a complex number — just as real numbers correspond to points on a line so complex numbers correspond to points in a plane:

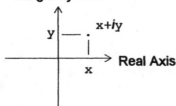

72

The point at coordinates (x,y) corresponds to the complex number $x+iy$ — the x-axis is the real axis and the y-axis is the imaginary axis. The extraordinary thing about complex numbers is that $i*i$ equals -1 but in other respects they act much like real numbers. The COMPLEX class defines a pair of constructors:

```
class COMPLEX {
public:
  COMPLEX(float = 0.0,float = 0.0);
  COMPLEX(const COMPLEX&);
    .
    .
private:
  float Real;
  float Imag;
};

COMPLEX::COMPLEX(float real,float imag) {
  Real = real;
  Imag = imag;
}

COMPLEX::COMPLEX(const COMPLEX& complex) {
  Real = complex.Real;
  Imag = complex.Imag;
}
```

The first constructor has both parameters optional and so can serve as a default constructor:

```
COMPLEX z;
```

Alternatively, both real and imaginary components can be supplied as parameters:

```
COMPLEX z(1.0,1.0);
```

Finally, if the first constructor is supplied with a single **float** parameter then it can act as a type conversion operator from type **float** to type COMPLEX. Type conversion operators are discussed further in chapter 9.

The second constructor copies the value of one COMPLEX object to another and so can act as a copy constructor:

```
COMPLEX z(1.0,1.0);
COMPLEX w = z;
```

Here the copy constructor is invoked to copy the value of z to w. Copy constructors are covered in more detail in the next chapter.

7.5 Temporary Objects

Temporary objects are usually created implicitly to hold the result of a function call. However, they may be created explicitly by directly invoking a constructor function. For example:

```
COMPLEX z = COMPLEX(1.0,1.0);
```

Here a temporary COMPLEX object is created and then used to initialize the z object — in some cases a compiler may be able to optimize the code so that a temporary object is not actually created but the effect is the same. This usage of temporary objects is similar to that involving the integer, floating-point and character constants that are directly supported by C++. A comparable example would be:

```
char letter = 'a';
```

Similarly, it may be helpful to explicitly generate temporary objects within an expression to serve as constants from a user-defined class.

7.6 Embedded Objects

In C++ one method of reusing software is to embed one object within another. The embedded object is simply listed as another data field in the class specification for the embedding object. For example, suppose an INNER class is declared:

```
class INNER {
    .
    .
};
```

Now an object of class INNER may be embedded within each object of class OUTER as follows:

```
class OUTER {
   .
   .
private:
   INNER Inner;
};
```

When an object has another object embedded within it, the creation and destruction procedures are modified slightly. The memory storage supplied to the OUTER object includes enough space to hold the INNER object as well as any other data that is required. The initialization and finalization procedures are also a bit more complicated. For creation of an OUTER object the steps are as follows:

1. Storage Allocation
2. INNER Object Initialization
3. OUTER Object Initialization

and similarly for destruction of the OUTER object the steps are:

1. OUTER Object Finalization
2. INNER Object Finalization
3. Storage Deallocation

In particular, note that when either the constructor or the destructor for the OUTER object is called the INNER object is in good health. The final point to explain is what happens when the INNER object is initialized — of course, a constructor for the INNER class is invoked but which one? If no constructor is explicitly specified then the default INNER() constructor is called. However, C++ supports the : notation to explicitly specify a constructor for the embedded object as part of the OUTER() constructor definition.

For example:

```
OUTER::OUTER(void) : Inner() {
   .
   .
}
```

Here the default INNER() constructor is explicitly invoked — the invocation appears between the : symbol and the opening brace of the OUTER() constructor. Naturally if the INNER class has other constructors besides the default one they may be chosen instead. For example, if there is an INNER(int) constructor declared then the following code is possible:

```
OUTER::OUTER(void) : Inner(123) {
   .
   .
}
```

The : notation also allows ordinary data fields within an object to be initialized before the constructor block is executed. For example:

```
class OUTER {
   .
   .
private:
   INNER Inner;
   int Data;
};

OUTER::OUTER(void) : Inner(123), Data(0) {
   .
   .
}
```

The individual items following the : symbol are separated by commas and the initialization values for ordinary data fields appear within parentheses.

7.7 The STRING Class

In C++ character strings are usually held in arrays with a terminating zero character — the STRING class will package a character string within an object and add some useful functions to manipulate strings. The class is fully developed throughout the next three chapters. This section considers the definition of a constuctor that initializes a STRING object given a C++ character pointer.

```
class STRING {
public:
    STRING(const char* = 0);
    void Print(void) const;
        .
        .
private:
    char String[100];
    int Length;
};
```

The constructor takes an optional char* parameter and so will act as a default constructor. The internal character array String is used to hold the string represented by the STRING object — the string will not have a terminating zero character and so the length is stored in the Length field. The constructor is defined as follows:

```
STRING::STRING(const char* string) {
    Length = 0;
    if (string)
        while (String[Length] = *string++)
            Length++;
    return;
}
```

The characters from the C++ string initializer are copied one at time to the String array until a terminating zero character is encountered. There is no check that the String array is big enough to hold the character string supplied — chapter 10 will fix this problem. The STRING class also provides a Print() function to display its string:

```
void STRING::Print(void) const {
  for (int i=0; i<Length; i++)
    cout << String[i];
  cout << '\n';
  return;
}
```

The following program demonstrates the STRING class:

```
#include "string.h"

int main(void) {
  STRING hello("Hello!");
  hello.Print();
  return 0;
}
```

The program creates a STRING object named hello and initializes it with the "Hello!" string — the Hello! message is then printed by invoking the Print() function of the hello object.

8. Regular Classes

This chapter discusses ways of making a C++ class as user-friendly as possible. The C++ language supports various built-in operations to handle the intrinsic character, integer and floating-point types — C++ classes can provide similar facilities for user-defined data types. Indeed some functions are essential for practically every class — a regular class is one which supports at least this minimal functionality. The relevant functions are the default constructor, the destructor, the copy constructor, the assignment operator, the equality operator and the inequality operator. C++ implicitly supplies basic versions of these functions if they are not explicitly defined. This chapter examines the individual functions in turn using the COMPLEX and STRING classes as examples.

8.1 User-Friendly Classes

The C++ language defines certain built-in operations for its basic data types. For example, a new integer variable can be created with a declaration statement:

```
int x;
```

Similarly, one variable can be assigned to another:

```
y = x;
```

C++ classes can provide similar functionality for user-defined data types — this helps to make objects much easier to work with. For example, the COMPLEX class introduced in the previous chapter is more user-friendly if it supports statements such as:

```
COMPLEX z;
```

and:

```
w = z;
```

These two statements should respectively declare an uninitialized COMPLEX object and assign the value of one

COMPLEX object to another. In such situations the C++ language supplies appropriate implicit functions for classes that do not define explicit versions — these implicit functions are discussed further in subsequent sections. Nonetheless, it is usually worthwhile defining the following functions explicitly:

1. Default constructor
2. Copy constructor
3. Assignment operator
4. Equality and inequality operators
5. Destructor

Any class which defines these functions (or accepts their implicit counterparts) is known as a 'regular' class — a regular class is typically quite user-friendly.

8.2 Default Constructor and Destructor

As discussed in the previous chapter, the implicit forms of the default ` constructor and destructor perform no noticeable processing. The default constructor is one which takes no parameters — a constructor with all its parameters optional can act as the default constructor. If any constructor is explicitly defined for a class then the implicit default constructor is not available. In particular this prevents the declaration of uninitialized objects and arrays of objects — the default constructor must be explicitly defined to enable these declarations.

8.3 Copy Constructor

A copy constructor is used to initialize a new object by copying the value of an existing object of the same class. The C++ language provides an implicit copy constructor which copies each data field in turn — if the class uses embedded objects then the procedure is applied recursively to each embedded object. The entire copy operation may reduce to a simple memory-to-memory copy.

The commonest form of copy constructor takes a constant reference to an existing object as a parameter — this object will not be modified by the construction process. For example, the DATE class can declare a copy constructor with the following function format:

```
DATE(const DATE&);
```

The parameter must be passed by reference since call-by-value semantics require the copy constructor to initialize the function parameter and this would lead to infinite recursion.

The COMPLEX class copy constructor is defined as follows:

```
class COMPLEX {
public:
  COMPLEX(const COMPLEX&);

      .

      .
private:
  float Real;
  float Imag;
};

COMPLEX::COMPLEX(const COMPLEX& complex) {
  Real = complex.Real;
  Imag = complex.Imag;
}
```

The action of this copy constructor is the same as that of the implicit version. Note that the Real and Imag fields of the existing object can be referenced within the constructor by applying the . operator to the function parameter. This is possible even though the fields are declared as private data — C++ supports encapsulation only at the class level and not at the object level. As another example here is a copy constructor for the STRING class:

```
STRING::STRING(const STRING& string) {
  Length = string.Length;
  for (int i=0; i<Length; i++)
    String[i] = string.String[i];
}
```

The COMPLEX and STRING class copy constructors both perform a shallow copy operation. A shallow copy simply copies the contents of one object to another — this is the only sort of copy operation available implicitly. However, if the original object contains a pointer field then a shallow copy just copies the pointer and so both the new and existing objects reference the same item through their pointers. This is depicted in the following figure:

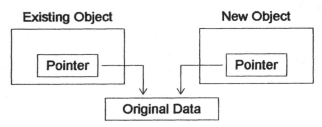

In contrast, a deep copy duplicates the data referenced by the pointer and the new object receives a pointer to the new copy of the data. If the data itself contains pointers this process can descend through several levels. The following figure demonstrates a deep copy involving one level of indirection:

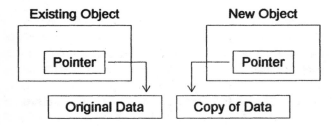

A compromise between shallow and deep copying options is to perform a shallow copy of a pointer but to maintain a reference count for the data pointed at. When the reference count drops to zero the data is no longer needed and may be discarded. These ideas are developed further in chapter 10 when the STRING class is updated to handle arbitrary length strings.

8.4 Assignment Operator

A feature of the C++ language is that the action of operators on user-defined types can be defined. This topic is covered in detail in the next chapter but this section and the next look at assignment and equality operators. The processing performed by the assignment is usually very similar to that performed by the copy constructor — the implicit version of the assignment operator just copies the contents of one object to another in much the same way as the implicit copy constructor. In fact, the main difference between a copy constructor and an assignment operator is that the former initializes a newly created object whilst the latter changes the value of an existing object. The assignment operator thus effectively combines the actions of the destructor and the copy constructor since assigning a new value to a object is a lot like erasing its contents and starting again. An assignment operator for the COMPLEX class may be defined as:

```
COMPLEX COMPLEX::operator=(COMPLEX complex) {
   Real = complex.Real;
   Imag = complex.Imag;
   return *this;
}
```

The function name is formed using the keyword **operator** and the = operator symbol. An operator function is invoked by applying the operator within an expression statement in the usual fashion. For example:

```
COMPLEX w, z;
w = z;
```

The expression statement invokes the assignment operator function for the COMPLEX class to copy the value of z to w. Note that the assignment operator returns a COMPLEX value so that assignments can be chained:

```
w = z = COMPLEX(1.0,1.0);
```

The above definition for the assignment operator causes the

function to be invoked using both call-by-value and return-by-value semantics — this involves a lot of copying and the process can be made more efficient by employing references:

```
COMPLEX&
COMPLEX::operator=(const COMPLEX& complex) {
  Real = complex.Real;
  Imag = complex.Imag;
  return *this;
}
```

Here is another example involving the STRING class:

```
STRING&
STRING::operator=(const STRING& string) {
  Length = string.Length;
  for (int i=0; i<Length; i++)
    String[i] = string.String[i];
  return *this;
}
```

8.5 Equality Operators

There are no implicit equality or inequality operators supplied by C++. Nonetheless, it can often be useful to define these functions explicitly since the notion of two objects being equal (or unequal) is usually sensible. For the COMPLEX class these operators may be defined as follows:

```
int
COMPLEX::operator==(const COMPLEX& complex) {
  return (Real==complex.Real
                && Imag==complex.Imag);
}
```

```
int
COMPLEX::operator!=(const COMPLEX& complex) {
  return !(*this == complex);
}
```

Both functions return a logical result that can be processed further within a logical expression. The inequality operator is defined in terms of the equality operator — this ensures that exactly one of the two operators returns true when comparing the same pair of COMPLEX objects. The use of these operators is intuitive as the following example demonstrates:

```
COMPLEX w;
COMPLEX z = COMPLEX(1.0,1.0);

if (w != z) {
    .
    .
}
```

The equality operators for the STRING class are a little more complicated:

```
int STRING::operator==(const STRING& string)
{
  if (Length. != string.Length)
    return 0;
  for (int i=0; i<Length; i++)
    if (String[i] != string.String[i])
      return 0;
  return 1;
}

int STRING::operator!=(const STRING& string)
{
  return !(*this == string);
}
```

Here two STRING objects are equal if and only if they hold identical character strings of the same length.

8.6 Dictionaries

A dictionary is a collection of entries each containing two elements:

1. Key
2. Value

For example, in a dictionary of words each key is a word and the corresponding value is its definition. The following code scans through the `dictionary` array of `ENTRY` objects looking for an entry which matches a given key:

```
ENTRY dictionary[100];
    .
    .
ENTRY entry = ENTRY(key);
int i = 0;
while (entry != dictionary[i])
   i++;
entry = dictionary[i];
```

There is no error checking to ensure that a valid entry actually exists in the `dictionary` array. Of course, the code requires the `ENTRY` class to be defined properly — to keep things simple both key and value elements in the `ENTRY` objects are integers.

```
class ENTRY {
public:
   ENTRY(int = 0,int = 0);
   ENTRY(const ENTRY&);
   ENTRY& operator=(const ENTRY&);
   int operator==(const ENTRY&);
   int operator!=(const ENTRY&);
      .
      .
private:
   int Key;
   int Value;
};
```

The first constructor builds an entry from a key-value pair — if only the `key` parameter is supplied as an argument then the `Value` field is filled with a null value.

```
ENTRY::ENTRY(int key,int value) {
   Key = key;
   Value = value;
}
```

The definitions for the copy constructor and the assignment operator are very similar:

```
ENTRY::ENTRY(const ENTRY& entry) {
   Key = entry.Key;
   Value = entry.Value;
}

ENTRY& ENTRY::operator=(const ENTRY& entry) {
   Key = entry.Key;
   Value = entry.Value;
   return *this;
}
```

Finally, the equality operators are defined as follows:

```
int ENTRY::operator==(const ENTRY& entry) {
   return (Key == entry.Key);
}

int ENTRY::operator!=(const ENTRY& entry) {
   return (Key != entry.Key);
}
```

The interesting point is that the equality operators work just with the Key fields of the ENTRY objects they compare whilst the copy constructor and the assignment operator duplicate both the Key and Value fields.

9. Operator Overloading

Operator overloading is an important feature of the C++ language — it allows the C++ operators to work with user-defined objects in much the same way as they do with variables of basic data types. To overload an operator a class must define a function which specifies the processing that is performed when the operator is applied to an object of the class. Most C++ operators can be overloaded. In general, the operator functions can produce any effect and return any result that is appropriate — the only restriction is that the overloaded versions must appear in expressions using the same syntax as their built-in counterparts. However, some operators require particular attention and they are discussed in detail in this chapter — such operators include the increment/decrement operators, the subscript operator, the function call operator and the pointer operator. Type conversion operators convert data from one type to another — operator overloading permits conversion to and from user-defined class types. Finally, the << and >> operators may be overloaded to provide consistent handling of stream input/output processing.

9.1 Operators and Operands

The previous chapter looked at three operators which can be overloaded by a class — these were the assignment operator, the equality operator and the inequality operator. Most C++ operators can be overloaded in this way. For binary operators the left-hand operand must be an object of the class defining the operator function whilst the right-hand operand is passed as a parameter to the function. For unary operators the object is the only operand and the operator function takes no parameters.

The INTEGER class provides a simple example of both binary and unary operators — the binary form of the overloaded – operator performs subtraction whilst the unary form performs negation. Each INTEGER object holds an integer Data field upon which the operations actually operate. The class specification is as follows:

```
class INTEGER {
public:
   INTEGER(int = 0);
   INTEGER operator-(INTEGER) const;
   INTEGER operator-(void) const;
   void Print(void) const;
private:
   int Data;
};
```

The constructor simply stores an integer data value within the object:

```
INTEGER::INTEGER(int data) {
   Data = data;
}
```

The overloaded operator functions have names composed of the keyword `operator` and the – operator symbol. The two functions are distinguished by their different parameter lists:

```
INTEGER
INTEGER::operator-(INTEGER integer) const
{
   return INTEGER(Data-integer.Data);
}

INTEGER INTEGER::operator-(void) const {
   return INTEGER(-Data);
}
```

In both cases a temporary `INTEGER` object is used to construct the result of the operator function. The `INTEGER` class also includes a `Print()` function to display the data it contains:

```
void INTEGER::Print(void) const {
   cout << Data << '\n';
}
```

The application of the INTEGER class is straightforward:

```
INTEGER i(7),j(3);
INTEGER k = i-j;
k.Print();
k = -j;
k.Print();
```

In the declaration statement for k the binary – operator function is invoked whilst in the assignment statement the unary – operator function is invoked instead. Hence the code prints the values 4 and -3 respectively.

9.2 Arithmetic Operators

For the COMPLEX class the arithmetic operators + (add), – (subtract), * (multiply) and / (divide) all need to be defined. In complex addition and subtraction the real and imaginary components of a complex number are treated separately. If z and w have the following complex values:

$$w == u + iv$$
$$z == x + iy$$

then

$$w + z == (u+x) + i(v+y)$$

This may be implemented in the COMPLEX class by overloading the + operator as follows:

```
COMPLEX
COMPLEX::operator+(const COMPLEX& z) const {
   return COMPLEX(Real+z.Real,Imag+z.Imag);
}
```

The subtraction operator is similar. For multiplication the relation $i*i == -1$ must be applied:

$$w*z == (u+iv)*(x+iy) == (u*x-v*y) + i(v*x+u*y)$$

The implementation of the overloaded * operator for

the COMPLEX class is consequently:

```
COMPLEX
COMPLEX::operator*(const COMPLEX& z) const {
  float real = Real*z.Real-Imag*z.Imag;
  float imag = Imag*z.Real+Real*z.Imag;
  return COMPLEX(real,imag);
}
```

The most complicated operation is complex division. To calculate w/z it is necessary to multiply both w and z by $x-iy$ (the conjugate of z):

$$w*(x-iy) == (u*x+v*y)+i(v*x-u*y)$$
$$z*(x-iy) == x*x+y*y$$

The denominator of the fraction $(x*x+y*y)$ is then real and it can be used to scale the real and imaginary components of the numerator appropriately. The implementation of the overloaded / operator for the COMPLEX class follows:

```
COMPLEX
COMPLEX::operator/(const COMPLEX& z) const {
  float real = Real*z.Real+Imag*z.Imag;
  float imag = Imag*z.Real-Real*z.Imag;
  float denom = z.Real*z.Real+z.Imag*z.Imag;
  if (denom == 0)
    exit(999);
  return COMPLEX(real/denom,imag/denom);
}
```

If the denominator of the division is zero the program terminates abruptly with a call to the exit() function. This function is declared in the stdlib.h system header and so the header file should be included by the source file for the COMPLEX class. Chapter 15 discusses another method of handling error conditions that involves C++ exceptions.

With the arithmetic operator functions defined, the COMPLEX class allows complex numbers to be manipulated easily — the functionality supplied by the COMPLEX class is analogous to the built-in support for real numbers that is provided by the intrinsic C++ type `float`. For example:

```
COMPLEX x(2.0);
COMPLEX y(3.0);
COMPLEX i(0.0,1.0);
COMPLEX z;
z = x+i*y;
```

The z object is assigned a complex value of $2+3i$ by this code. Sections 9.7 and 9.8 discuss in more detail the subject of mixing real and complex data within an expression.

9.3 Subscript Operator

The subscript operator `[]` is typically overloaded to select an individual item from a collection of items. A simple example is provided by the STRING class introduced in the previous two chapters:

```
char STRING::operator[](int i) {
if (i<0 || i>=Length)
  return 0;
else
  return String[i];
}
```

The subscript selects a character from the string held by the object — if the subscript falls outside the range of the string array then a zero character is returned.

A related application is to provide bounds checking for an array — in C++ if an array subscript tries to reference an element beyond the bounds of the array the result is often the modification of some unrelated piece of data that is stored in memory adjacent to the array. This sort of error can be very hard to trace — the ARRAY class checks that a subscript is within range before permitting the corresponding element to be referenced. As defined here the ARRAY class contains a `float` array and allows the subscript of the first element to be set by the class constructor — arrays in C++

are intrinsically zero-based but one-based arrays are sometimes useful. The ARRAY class specification follows:

```
class ARRAY {
public:
  ARRAY(int,int = 0);
  float& operator[](int);
private:
  float Array[100];
  int Length;
  int Base;
};
```

The constructor simply stores its parameters in the Length and Base fields — a check is also performed on the requested array length.

```
ARRAY::ARRAY(int length,int base) {
  if (length<0 || length>=100)
    exit(999);
  Length = length;
  Base = base;
}
```

The overloaded [] operator performs most of the work — it checks each subscript against the bounds of the array and if it is within bounds then a reference to the appropriate element is returned.

```
float& ARRAY::operator[](int i) {
  i -= Base;
  if (i<0 || i>=Length)
    exit(999);
  return Array[i];
}
```

Here is an example which uses the ARRAY class:

```
ARRAY Months(12,1);
Months[6] = 0.0;
Months[13] = 0.0;
```

The Months array contains twelve elements and the first element is Months[1]. Hence the first assignment statement references the array element for June whilst the second causes the program to abort with an array bounds error.

9.4 Increment and Decrement Operators

The overloading of the increment and decrement operators is complicated by the fact that they occur in two forms:

1. Prefix form
2. Postfix form

In prefix form the operators precede their operand whilst in postfix form they follow it. When these operators are overloaded, the two forms are distinguished by allotting the postfix operator function a dummy integer parameter — the prefix operator function takes no parameters. The INTEGER class from section 9.1 can be extended to support both forms of increment operator with the following modifications:

```
class INTEGER {
public:
   INTEGER operator++(void);
   INTEGER operator++(int);
     .
     .
     .
};
```

The prefix form of the operator is overloaded as follows:

```
INTEGER INTEGER::operator++(void) {
   return INTEGER(++Data);
}
```

The postfix form is implemented in a similar fashion:

```
INTEGER INTEGER::operator++(int junk) {
   return INTEGER(Data++);
}
```

The operators are applied in the usual way:

```
INTEGER i(0);
++i;
i++;
i.Print();
```

This code prints out the value 2 as expected.

9.5 Function Call Operator

The function call operator `()` is interesting in that it can take any number of parameters — the operator can be overloaded several times by the same class as long as the parameter list for each version is different. One possible application is to extract a substring by providing the start and stop positions within a larger string as parameters:

```
STRING
STRING::operator()(int start,int stop) const
{
  int length = stop-start;
  const char* string = String+start;
  return STRING(string,length);
}
```

The function performs no error-checking and relies on a STRING constructor which takes two parameters:

```
STRING::STRING(const char* string,int length)
{
  Length = length;
  for (int i=0; i<Length; i++)
    String[i] = *string++;
}
```

The substring operator is easy to use:

```
STRING hippo("Hippo");
STRING hi = hippo(0,2);
hi.Print();
```

Another possible application for an overloaded function call operator is to reference elements within a multi-dimensional array. For example, the MATRIX class implements a two-dimensional array:

```
class MATRIX {
public:
  MATRIX(int);
  float& operator()(int,int);
private:
  float Array[100];
  int Dimension;
};
```

The constructor accepts the second dimension of the matrix as a parameter:

```
MATRIX::MATRIX(int dimension) {
  Dimension = dimension;
}
```

The () operator acts as a subscript operator which takes two parameters:

```
float& MATRIX::operator()(int i,int j) {
  return Array[i*Dimension+j];
}
```

The elements of the two-dimensional array are stored within the memory space allocated to the one-dimensional array field Array. The elements for the first row (i==0) of the matrix are followed immediately by those for the second row (i==1) and so on. As described in section 3.8 this layout mimics the way in which C++ stores multi-dimensional arrays.

9.6 Pointer Operator

The overloading of the pointer operator -> is handled in rather an unusual way. The first action is to invoke the overloaded operator function — the object associated with the function call is the left-hand operand of the -> operator.

For example:

```
class POINTER {
public:
  INTEGER* operator->(void);
    .
    .
};

POINTER pointer;
pointer->Print();
```

Here the -> operator function for the `pointer` object is invoked. The function must take no parameters and return one of the following:

1. a pointer
2. an object of a class that overloads the -> operator

In the first case the built-in -> operator is applied using the returned pointer and the original right-hand operand. In the above example the `Print()` function of an `INTEGER` object is invoked.

In the second case the whole procedure is applied recursively using the new object in place of the original operand. For example:

```
class SLAVE {
public:
  INTEGER* operator->(void);
    .
    .
};

class MASTER {
public:
  SLAVE operator->(void);
    .
    .
};
```

The following code provides a demonstration:

```
MASTER pointer;
pointer->Print();
```

Here the MASTER object supplies a SLAVE object which returns a pointer to an INTEGER object. The Print() function is then called for the INTEGER object.

The point of overloading the -> operator is that some user-defined processing (often error checking) can be performed before the pointer is dereferenced. Objects with an overloaded -> operator are consequently known as 'smart pointers' — this topic is discussed further in chapter 14.

9.7 Type Conversion Operators

Type conversion operators are closely related to type casts. The C++ language supplies type conversion operators to cast between the basic types:

```
float x;
int count = int(x);
```

C++ will sometimes apply type conversion operators implicitly — in particular this is true for type conversion operators that are user-defined. There are essentially two ways to provide a user-defined type conversion operator — both involve class functions:

1. A constructor
2. An overloaded operator

In the first case the constructor should take a single parameter — the conversion is from the type of the parameter to the class type. For example:

```
class COMPLEX {
public:
  COMPLEX(float = 0.0,float = 0.0);
    .
    .
};
```

99

If the above constructor is supplied with a single **float** argument it will act as a type conversion operator from type **float** to type COMPLEX. This conversion will be applied implicitly by C++:

```
COMPLEX z = 2.0;
```

Here the floating-point value 2.0 is implicitly converted to a COMPLEX object. Similarly, real and complex numbers can be mixed in an expression:

```
COMPLEX i = COMPLEX(0.0,1.0);
COMPLEX z = i*3+2;
```

The integer values 3 and 2 are converted to floating-point values by a built-in conversion and then to temporary COMPLEX objects — the C++ language will perform at most one built-in conversion and one user-defined conversion on each piece of data. Note that the overloaded * and + operators must be provided with a COMPLEX object as their left-hand operand — the next section demonstrates a technique to overcome this restriction.

The second kind of user-defined type conversion operator is defined as an overloaded operator. For example:

```
class COMPLEX {
public:
  operator float(void) const;
  .
  .
};

COMPLEX::operator float(void) const {
  return (float)sqrt(Real*Real+Imag*Imag);
}
```

The operator function returns the modulus of the complex number held by the COMPLEX object. Note that the return type is not specified since it is implicit in the function name — the function performs a type conversion from COMPLEX to **float**. The result is calculated using the sqrt()

function which is declared in the `math.h` system header. The type conversion will be applied implicitly in code such as the following:

```
COMPLEX z;
float modulus = z;
```

Care should be exercised when defining type conversion operators since they be may applied implicitly in unexpected circumstances. For example, if the + operator is overloaded by the COMPLEX class and type conversions from `float` to COMPLEX and back both exist, then the following addition expression is ambiguous:

```
float x;
COMPLEX z;
z+x;
```

The two possible interpretations of z+x are:

1. Convert z to type `float` and add x
2. Convert x to type COMPLEX and add z

However, the expression x+z uniquely specifies the first option even though there is a `float` to COMPLEX conversion available.

Of course, explicit type conversions involving user-defined functions are also possible. For example:

```
z = COMPLEX(x);
x = float(z);
```

Alternatively using casting notation:

```
z = (COMPLEX)x;
x = (float)z;
```

9.8 Friend Functions

The final point about operator overloading is that it may be performed using global friend functions instead of functions belonging directly to a class. For a unary operator the operand is passed as the lone parameter of the friend function, whilst for a binary operator the left- and right-hand operands appear as the first and second parameters respectively — the left-hand operand need not be an object. However, in other respects operator overloading with friend functions is very similar to using class functions. For example:

```
class COMPLEX {
friend COMPLEX operator+(float,const COMPLEX&);
   .
   .
   .
};

COMPLEX operator+(float x,const COMPLEX& z) {
   return COMPLEX(x+z.Real,z.Imag);
}
```

The overloaded + operator function belonging to the COMPLEX class and the above friend function together permit the following pair of addition expressions involving a mixture of real and complex numbers:

```
COMPLEX z;
COMPLEX i(0.0,1.0);
z = i+2;
z = 2+i;
```

The first addition invokes the class function whilst the second invokes the friend function.

Friend functions are particularly useful when the << and >> operators are overloaded to perform input and output — in this situation the stream object should be the left-hand operand and so overloading with a function of another class is not possible. The approach provides a more elegant solution to input/output processing than does the definition of assorted functions such as Print() for each class. For example, the STRING class can replace the Print() function defined in section 7.7 with an overloaded << operator function.

The necessary modifications are as follows:

```
class STRING {
friend
ostream& operator<<(ostream&,const STRING&);
   .
   .
};

ostream&
operator<<(ostream& out,const STRING& string)
{
   for (int i=0; i<string.Length; i++)
     out << string.String[i];
   return out;
}
```

A string can then be displayed with code such as the following:

```
STRING hello("Hello");
cout << hello << '\n';
```

An output operator for the COMPLEX class may be similarly defined:

```
class COMPLEX {
friend
ostream& operator<<(ostream&,const COMPLEX&);
   .
   .
};

ostream&
operator<<(ostream& out,const COMPLEX& z) {
   out << '(';
   out << z.Real;
   out << ',';
   out << z.Imag;
   out << ')';
   return out;
}
```

To display the complex number held by a COMPLEX object the following code may be used:

```
COMPLEX z;
cout << "z = " << z << '\n';
```

The output statement will print:

```
z = (0,0)
```

10. Dynamic Objects

The global, local and temporary objects considered in earlier chapters are examples of static objects — the lifespan of these objects is determined at compile time. By contrast dynamic objects are explicitly created and destroyed at run-time using the new and delete operators. Furthermore, storage space for static objects is typically allocated on the stack whilst that for dynamic objects is taken from a pool of free memory. Indeed the creation and destruction of dynamic C++ objects is intimately linked with the management of memory storage allocated to these objects. This chapter examines two implementations of the STRING class as examples of programming with dynamic objects. The overloading of the new and delete operators is also discussed.

10.1 Static and Dynamic Objects

The previous chapters have dealt with C++ objects that may be categorized as follows:

1. Global Objects
2. Local Objects
3. Temporary Objects

Objects of these three sorts may be described as static objects in the sense that their lifespan is fixed at compile time — global objects exist throughout the entire execution of the program, local objects exist whilst the block statement in which they are declared is processed and temporary objects exist during the evaluation of an expression. The storage space for static objects is typically allocated on the stack — the stack is a special area of memory reserved by the program and the total storage available within the stack is often limited. The operation of the stack is intimately tied with function invocations — the figure on the following page illustrates the state of the stack before, during and after a function call.

Before Call	During Call	After Call
Allocated Storage	Allocated Storage	Allocated Storage
Available Storage	Current Stack Frame	Available Storage
	Available Storage	

A chunk of memory to hold the current stack frame is allocated for the duration of the function call. The stack frame contains such items as the function parameters, local and temporary variables as well as the function return address — the return address indicates the point in the program where execution should resume once the function returns. When function calls are nested, new stack frames are added as the nested functions are entered and lost as the functions return. Hence the amount of storage allocated on the stack grows and shrinks as the program executes.

In addition to static objects C++ also provides dynamic objects — the lifespan of a dynamic object is determined at run-time and is under complete control of the programmer. The creation and destruction of a dynamic object are not directly related to function invocations and so storage for a dynamic object cannot be allocated on the stack. Instead storage for dynamic objects is allocated from a pool of free memory which is typically much larger than the stack — indeed the dynamic memory pool will usually contain all the remaining memory not assigned to the stack or otherwise required by the system.

The operators `new` and `delete` are provided to create and destroy dynamic objects. The process is very similar to that for static objects — during creation the following two steps are performed:

1. Storage Allocation
2. Object Initialization

and during destruction the steps are:

1. Object Finalization
2. Storage Deallocation

As with static objects, dynamic objects are initialized by invoking their constructor and they are finalized by invoking their destructor. The only difference between static and dynamic objects is that the former have storage allocated on the stack whilst the latter have storage allocated from the free memory pool. Here is an example of creating and destroying a dynamic DATE object:

```
DATE* today. = (DATE*) new DATE;
    .
    .
delete today;
```

The **new** keyword is followed by a type name and generates a dynamic object of the specified class — the operator returns a **void** pointer which must be cast to a pointer of the appropriate type before being assigned to a pointer variable. The dynamic object continues to exist until the **delete** operator is applied to its pointer — at this point the object is destroyed. Note that applying the **delete** operator to a null pointer is allowed and has no effect.

Incidentally, the **new** and **delete** operators also work with basic C++ types so the following code processes a dynamic integer variable:

```
int* count = (int*) new int;
    .
    .
delete count;
```

A dynamic object (or variable) is never referenced by name and is always manipulated through a pointer. For example:

```
DATE* yesterday = (DATE*) new DATE;
yesterday->SetDate(1,1,1970);
```

This code sets the value of the dynamic DATE object by applying the -> operator to its yesterday pointer. The information could also be passed directly to the object's constructor:

```
DATE* yesterday = (DATE*) new DATE(1,1,1970);
```

Here the yesterday variable receives a pointer to a DATE object which has already been initialized.

10.2 Dynamic Arrays

C++ also supports the creation of dynamic arrays — the element type may be either built-in or user-defined. The syntax is straightforward:

```
int* array = (int*) new int[10];
    .
    .
delete [] array;
```

This code processes an array of ten integer elements. Note the use of the [] marker with the delete operator — this tells C++ that it must determine the length of the array to be deleted. To enable this operation C++ stores the length of each array as it is created — the [] mechanism means that this value need only be stored for arrays and not for every dynamic object. Nonetheless, the following (hypothetical) notation would be nicer:

```
delete array[];
```

Anyway, when a dynamic array is created the default constructor is invoked to initialize each array element — unlike dynamic objects it is not possible to supply arguments to each array element constructor.

The STRING class defined in section 7.7 used a static character array to hold its string — the class is updated here to handle arbitrary length strings by replacing the static array with a dynamic array. The class specification follows:

```
class STRING {
public:
  STRING(const char* = 0);
  STRING(const STRING&);
  ~STRING(void);
  STRING& operator=(const STRING&);
  STRING operator+(const STRING&) const;
    .
    .
private:
  char* String;
  int Length;
};
```

The first constructor creates a dynamic character array just large enough to hold the string passed in as a parameter:

```
STRING::STRING(const char* string) {
  Length = 0;
  if (!string) return;
  const char* letter = string;
  while (*letter++) Length++;
  if (!Length) return;
  String = (char*) new char[Length];
  for (int i=0; i<Length; i++)
    String[i] = string[i];
}
```

The copy constructor is similar but the Length field can be copied directly from the existing object:

```
STRING::STRING(const STRING& string) {
  Length = string.Length;
  if (!Length) return;
  String = (char*) new char[Length];
  for (int i=0; i<Length; i++)
    String[i] = string.String[i];
}
```

The copy constructor performs a deep copy as discussed in section 8.3 — an alternative approach which employs reference counting is presented in the next section.

The STRING class destructor is responsible for destroying the character array if it exists:

```
STRING::~STRING(void) {
  if (Length)
    delete [] String;
}
```

The assignment operator for the class combines the processing performed by the destructor and the copy constructor. However, the function must first check that the STRING object is not being assigned to itself — without this check the object's dynamic character array would be deleted before it could be copied.

```
STRING&
STRING::operator=(const STRING& string) {
  if (this == &string)
    return *this;
  if (Length)
    delete [] String;
  Length = string.Length;
  if (!Length)
    return *this;
  String = (char*) new char[Length];
  for (int i=0; i<Length; i++)
    String[i] = string.String[i];
  return *this;
}
```

Finally, the + operator is overloaded to permit string concatenation — the result of applying the concatenation operator to a pair of strings is another string that contains the original two strings one after the other. The STRING class implements the concatenation operator as follows:

```
STRING
STRING::operator+(const STRING& right) const
{
  int length = Length + right.Length;
  if (!length)
    return STRING();
  char* string = (char*) new char[length+1];
  for (int i=0; i<Length; i++)
    string[i] = String[i];
  for (i=0; i<right.Length; i++)
    string[i+Length] = right.String[i];
  string[length] = 0;
  STRING leftright(string);
  delete [] string;
  return leftright;
}
```

The left- and right-hand STRING operands of the overloaded operator have their String fields copied to a dynamic character array. This array is then used to construct a new STRING object which is returned as the result of the concatenation. Here is some code to test the class:

```
STRING good("Good");
STRING bye("bye");
STRING goodbye = good+bye;
cout << goodbye << '\n';
```

The STRING class needs a friend function to overload the << operator — see section 9.8 for a suitable definition.

10.3 Reference Counting

An alternative method of implementing the STRING class is to define a related TEXT class to hold the actual character strings — each STRING object contains a pointer to an associated TEXT object. The method involves shallow copying of STRING objects — see section 8.3 for further details on shallow and deep copying.

Each TEXT object maintains a reference count which indicates how many STRING objects are currently referencing it — whenever the reference count drops to zero the TEXT object destroys itself. The TEXT class specification is as follows:

```
class TEXT {
public:
  TEXT(const char*);
  ~TEXT(void);
  void Acquire(void);
  void Release(void);
private:
  char* String;
  int Length;
  int Count;
};
```

The TEXT constructor stores the string parameter and sets the Count field to 1 indicating that one STRING object references this TEXT object:

```
TEXT::TEXT(const char* string) {
  Count = 1;
  Length = 0;
  if (!string) return;
  const char* letter = string;
  while (*letter++) Length++;
  if (!Length) return;
  String = (char*) new char[Length];
  for (int i=0; i<Length; i++)
    String[i] = string[i];
}
```

The destructor releases the dynamic character array if it exists:

```
TEXT::~TEXT(void) {
  if (Length)
    delete [] String;
}
```

The Acquire() and Release() functions respectively increment and decrement the TEXT object's reference count:

```
void TEXT::Acquire(void) {
  Count++;
}

void TEXT::Release(void) {
  if (--Count) return;
  delete this;
}
```

The Release() function is responsible for destroying the TEXT object when its reference count drops to zero.

The STRING class specification follows:

```
class STRING {
public:
  STRING(const char* = 0);
  STRING(const STRING&);
  ~STRING(void);
  STRING& operator=(const STRING&);
    .
    .
private:
  TEXT* Text;
};
```

The first constructor creates an associated dynamic TEXT object:

```
STRING::STRING(const char* string) {
  Text = (TEXT*) new TEXT(string);
}
```

The destructor releases the reference to the TEXT object:

```
STRING::~STRING(void) {
  Text->Release();
}
```

If the STRING object is holding the last reference to

the TEXT object when the destructor is invoked, the TEXT object will also destroy itself.

The copy constructor duplicates only the pointer to the TEXT object. However, the reference count for the TEXT object is incremented by calling its Acquire() function:

```
STRING::STRING(const STRING& string) {
  Text = string.Text;
  Text->Acquire();
}
```

The assignment operator combines the actions of destructor and copy constructor — as in the previous implementation of the STRING class, a check must be made for self-assignment to guard against releasing (and possibly destroying) the TEXT object before it is acquired again.

```
STRING&
STRING::operator=(const STRING& string) {
  if (Text == string.Text)
    return *this;
  Text->Release();
  Text = string.Text;
  Text->Acquire();
  return *this;
}
```

To display the string represented by a STRING object the two classes should define friend functions:

```
ostream&
operator<<(ostream& out,const STRING& string)
{
  return (out << *(string.Text));
}

ostream&
operator<<(ostream& out,const TEXT& text) {
  for (int i=0; i<text.Length; i++)
    out << text.String[i];
  return out;
}
```

10.4 Memory Management

Each C++ implementation supplies default versions of the **new** and **delete** operators, but a class can overload these operators much like any others. The first parameter of the overloaded **new** operator must be of type `size_t` — this type is defined in the `stddef.h` system header. The overloaded **delete** operator may accept either one or two parameters (but both variants are not allowed in the same class) — the first parameter is a **void** pointer whilst the second is of type `size_t`. Additional parameters for the **new** operator are considered in the next section whilst the second parameter to the **delete** operator is discussed further in chapter 13. For both the **new** and **delete** operators, the `size_t` parameter indicates how many bytes of memory should be allocated or deallocated. The **new** operator must return a **void** pointer type and the **delete** operator should return no result.

The POOL class will serve as an example of overloading the **new** and **delete** operators. This class acquires a large pool of memory and then allocates memory from the pool whenever new POOL objects are created. The specification for the POOL class follows:

```
class POOL {
public:
  void* operator new(size_t);
  void operator delete(void*);

    .
    .
private:
  static POOL* Pool;
  int Free;
  int Data;
};
```

The static `Pool` field belongs to the POOL class as a whole and it is used to detect the creation of the first POOL object.

115

The field is initialized in a global statement that is processed prior to execution of the `main()` function:

```
POOL* POOL::Pool = 0;
```

When the overloaded **new** operator is invoked, it checks the `Pool` field and if it is zero the class memory pool is acquired:

```
void* POOL::operator new (size_t size) {
  if (!Pool) {
    Pool = (POOL*) ::new char[100*size];
    for (int i=0; i<100; i++)
      Pool[i].Free = 1;
  }
  for (int i=0; i<100; i++)
    if (Pool[i].Free) break;
  if (i<100) {
    Pool[i].Free = 0;
    return Pool+i;
  }
  return 0;
}
```

The global **new** operator is invoked to allocate a memory pool by creating a dynamic character array. Since each element of the character array will hold exactly one byte of data, the allocated storage contains (100*size) bytes of memory — this is just big enough to support a hundred POOL objects. The global operator is specified by prefixing the **new** keyword with the :: operator as discussed in the next section. The static Pool field effectively acts as an array of POOL objects — each element initially has its Free field set to true to indicate that no dynamic POOL objects have been created. At each invocation of the **new** operator, the elements of the array are scanned to find an unallocated object — the Free field of the new object is set to false.

The overloaded `delete` operator returns an object to the pool by setting its `Free` field back to true:

```
void POOL::operator delete(void* pointer) {
  POOL* object = (POOL*) pointer;
  object->Free = 1;
}
```

10.5 Global `new` and `delete` Operators

If a class does not overload the `new` and `delete` operators, the global `new` and `delete` operator functions provided by the C++ implementation are invoked instead. The global operators are always available (even within a class with overloaded versions) by prefixing the `new` and `delete` keywords with the `::` operator. It is possible to redefine the global operators with user-defined functions. The global `new` operator has an initial parameter of type `size_t` whilst the global `delete` operator has a single parameter of `void` pointer type. Overloaded versions of the global `new` function can accept any number of additional parameters (as can overloaded `new` operators defined by a class) — these parameters are supplied in a parenthesized list following the `new` keyword. For example:

```
DATE* today = (DATE*) new (1000) DATE(1,1,1970);
```

The value `1000` appears as the second parameter to the `new` operator function whilst the other parameters (placed in parentheses following the `DATE` type name) are passed directly to the constructor of the dynamic object. One possible use for the additional parameters to the `new` operator could be to place objects from different classes in separate memory pools.

11. Concrete Classes

Concrete classes are designed to provide some specific functionality — the COMPLEX and STRING classes from the previous chapters are examples of concrete classes. This chapter looks at several more concrete classes which embody the standard data structures commonly provided by a utility class library — the class oriented nature of C++ is especially well-suited to the implementation of these data structures. Lists, trees and heaps are all considered as examples of hierarchical data structures — such a structure organises its data into a number of logical levels arranged in a hierarchy below the root element. The manipulation of a hierarchical data structure can be considerably easier if recursive programming techniques are applied.

11.1 Class Categories

The remaining chapters in the book look at the various categories of C++ class:

1. Concrete Classes
2. Template Classes
3. Base Classes
4. Interface Classes
5. Exception Classes

All the examples of classes described in earlier chapters are concrete classes. They are designed for some specific purpose — typical examples of concrete classes are the utility classes found in a class library. This chapter looks at utility classes for handling lists, trees and heaps. C++ templates allow several classes to be defined using a single template class as a blue-print — the following chapter deals with template classes in detail. Base classes (or inheritable classes) are not complete classes in the same way that concrete classes are — they provide some general functionality but in most cases this must be extended with the definition of a concrete class derived from the base class. Chapter 13 explains inheritance in C++ and describes the process of constructing base and derived classes. An interface class is an extreme variety of inheritable class that contains no functionality at all — its purpose is to specify the precise format of the functions which are available for communicating with objects of any concrete class derived from the interface class. Chapter 14 covers interface classes and their connection to software components. Finally, exception classes are supported by C++ as a means of structured error handling — chapter 15 discusses C++ exceptions and the related keywords `try`, `throw` and `catch`.

11.2 Hierarchical Data Structures

In a flat data structure the individual elements are all positioned at the same logical level and they can be reached directly from the root of the data structure. For example, a single-dimensional array is a flat data structure — given the array name each of the elements can be referenced using the `[]` operator. The following figure demonstrates the idea for an array `x` containing four elements:

Root of Data Structure

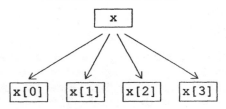

The root of the data structure and the individual elements are collectively known as nodes. In a flat data structure there is a clear distinction between the root node (which represents the whole structure) and the other nodes (which represent individual elements). However, in a hierarchical data structure this distinction is blurred and any node can act as the root node of a sub-structure. For example, a two-dimensional array may be regarded as a hierarchical data structure — the two-by-two array `x[2][2]` is depicted

120

as such in the following figure:

Root of Data Structure

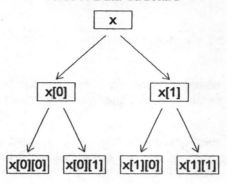

At the top level the root node refers to the array as a whole, at the middle level each node refers to a row within the array and finally at the bottom level each node refers to an element within a row. In other words the root node represents a two-dimensional array, the internal nodes represent one-dimensional arrays and the terminal nodes represent zero-dimensional arrays. So every node represents an array and points to sub-arrays within that array — only the dimension of the arrays decreases as the structure is descended. Hence all nodes in a hierarchical structure are in some sense indistinguishable — at every level each node acts as the root of a sub-structure which has essentially the same form as at any other level.

This chapter looks at three types of hierarchical data structure (lists, trees and heaps) and discusses their implementation as concrete C++ classes which could form part of a utility class library.

11.3 Lists

Lists are similar data structures to arrays and contain a number of items. Since these items can themselves be lists, a list is a hierarchical data structure. However, the essential functionality provided by a list can be examined by ignoring the type of each item and treating the list as a flat data structure. The items within a list are ordered from head to tail as shown in the following figure:

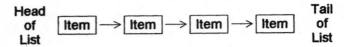

Items can be added or removed at any point in the list and the existing elements retain their relative ordering during this operation.

A C++ list is typically implemented using pointers to link the individual items together. An extra header item can be added at the head of the list — its only purpose is to avoid having an empty list. The item at the tail of the list sets its pointer to zero to indicate that no more items follow. For example, here is a list with two items:

The earth symbol is employed to denote a null pointer. The ITEM class implements a list item and has the following specification:

```
class ITEM {
public:
  ITEM(void);
  void Add(ITEM*);
  void Remove(ITEM*);
    .
    .
private:
  ITEM* Next;
  void* Data;
};
```

The Next pointer creates the link to the next item in the list.

The default constructor simply zeroes the Next field — this is useful when creating the header for an empty list. Each ITEM object also contains a **void** pointer named Data — this allows the item to hold any type of data. In particular, for a hierarchical list structure the Data field could refer to an entire sub-list.

The Add() function takes a pointer to an existing item in the list and positions the new item after this item.

```
void ITEM::Add(ITEM* previous) {
  Next = previous->Next;
  previous->Next = this;
}
```

The following figure illustrates the situation when Item_C has been placed after Item_A in the list depicted on the left:

The Remove() function is similar to the Add() function:

```
void ITEM::Remove(ITEM* previous) {
  previous->Next = Next;
  Next = 0;
}
```

The problem with this solution is that a pointer to the previous element must be supplied when an item is removed from the list. However, each list item is an object and objects should be delegated power whenever possible. The provision of a Previous field in addition to the Next field enables an ITEM object to determine its predecessor during removal. The resulting list is known as a doubly-linked list:

To make the code more symmetrical a trailer item could be added at the tail of the list:

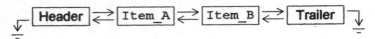

However, a simpler alternative is to wrap the pointers around and form a circularly linked list — the header then acts as a trailer too:

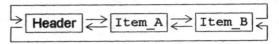

The updated ITEM class specification follows:

```
class ITEM {
public:
  ITEM(void);
  void Add(ITEM*);
  void Remove(void);
    .
    .
private:
  ITEM* Next;
  ITEM* Previous;
  void* Data;
};
```

The default constructor sets the Next and Previous fields to point to the item itself:

```
ITEM::ITEM(void) {
  Next = Previous = this;
}
```

The Add() function must maintain the pointer links in both directions:

```
void ITEM::Add(ITEM* previous) {
  Next = previous->Next;
  Previous = Next->Previous;
  Previous->Next = this;
  Next->Previous = this;
}
```

The Remove() function now does not need to be passed a pointer to the previous item in the list:

```
void ITEM::Remove(void) {
    Previous->Next = Next;
    Next->Previous = Previous;
    Next = Previous = this;
}
```

Note that these functions rely heavily on the fact that C++ supports encapsulation only at the class level.

11.4 Recursive Programming

A recursive function is one which invokes itself — each recursive function comprises two parts:

1. A nested function call
2. A terminating condition

The first part provides the recursion whilst the second part prevents the function repeatedly invoking itself forever — without the terminating condition the result is infinite recursion and the program will eventually abort as it runs out of stack space.

A simple example of recursion is the Factorial() function which calculates the product of its integer argument and all smaller integers:

```
Factorial(1) == 1
Factorial(2) == 2*1 == 2
Factorial(3) == 3*2*1 == 6
Factorial(4) == 4*3*2*1 == 24
    .
    .
```

The recursive definition of this function follows:

```
int Factorial(int n) {
    if (n == 1)
        return 1;
    return (n*Factorial(n-1));
}
```

The recursive function call is provided by the statement:

```
return (n*Factorial(n-1));
```

The conditional statement:

```
if (n == 1)
    return 1;
```

checks for the terminating condition n==1.

Suppose the function is invoked by the following code:

```
int answer = Factorial(4);
```

Here a nested series of calls to the Factorial() function occurs with n==4, n==3, n==2 and finally n==1. The results passed back as the nested functions return are 1, 2, 6, and finally 24.

In some cases the recursive definition of a function has an iterative counterpart. For example:

```
int Factorial(int n) {
    int factorial = 1;
    for (int i=1; i<=n; i++)
        factorial *= i;
    return factorial;
}
```

The iterative solution is more efficient because it avoids the overhead of several function invocations. However, a recursive solution is often a lot simpler to code and this is especially true for the hierarchical data structures (trees and heaps) that are discussed in the next two sections.

11.5 Trees

A tree is a classic example of a hierarchical data structure. It has a root node from which branches lead to nodes at the first level, each of these nodes is the root for its own sub-tree and more branches lead to nodes at the second level — the structure is repeated until at the final level are the leaf nodes. A binary tree supports just two branches from each node — the following figure demonstrates the layout of such a tree:

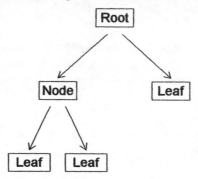

Each node holds pointers to its left and right sub-trees — either of these pointers may be null to indicate that the sub-tree is empty. If both pointers are null then the node is a leaf node.

The NODE class will implement the nodes within a tree structure. Each NODE object contains Left and Right pointer fields to refer to its sub-trees — an integer Data field is also associated with the node.

```
class NODE {
public:
   NODE(int);
   void Add(NODE*&,NODE* = 0);
   void Remove(NODE*&);
   NODE* Find(int);
      .
      .
private:
   NODE* Left;
   NODE* Right;
   NODE* Parent;
   int Data;
};
```

The `Parent` field points to the node immediately above the current node in the tree structure — it serves the same function that the `Previous` field did in the `ITEM` class of section 11.3, namely to allow a `NODE` object to remove itself from the tree.

The constructor sets the `Data` field using its parameter and simply zeroes the `Left`, `Right` and `Parent` pointers — the pointer fields are properly initialized when the node is added to a tree.

```
NODE::NODE(int data) {
   Left = Right = Parent = 0;
   Data = data;
}
```

New nodes will be placed in the tree acording to the value of their `Data` field. If their data value is less than that of the root node they will be placed in the left sub-tree of the root — otherwise they will be placed in the right sub-tree of the root. This decision process is applied recursively at each level within the tree — the `Add()` function is therefore easy to implement as a recursive function:

```
void NODE::Add(NODE*& root,NODE* parent) {
   if (!root) {
      root = this;
      Left = Right = 0;
      Parent = parent;
   }
   else if (Data < root->Data)
      Add(root->Left,root);
   else
      Add(root->Right,root);
}
```

There are two interesting points concerning the `Add()` function — firstly, the `Parent` field of the tree's root node will be set to null by the optional parameter value and secondly, the `root` parameter is passed as a reference to a pointer so that the pointer value can be modified.

A new NODE is inserted into the tree by passing a pointer to the tree's root node:

```
NODE* nodes[5];
for (int i=0; i<5; i++)
   nodes[i] = new NODE(i);
NODE* root = 0;
nodes[3]->Add(root);
nodes[1]->Add(root);
nodes[4]->Add(root);
nodes[2]->Add(root);
nodes[0]->Add(root);
```

This code builds the following tree structure:

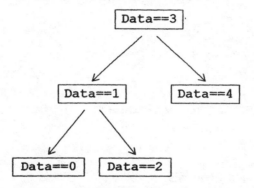

The Remove() function has the following definition:

```
void NODE::Remove(NODE*& root) {
   if (!Parent)
      root = 0;
   else if (Parent->Left == this)
      Parent->Left = 0;
   else
      Parent->Right = 0;
   Parent = 0;
}
```

This definition allows an entire sub-tree to be removed by

invoking the function on the NODE object at the root of the sub-tree.

The ordering of nodes within the tree allows a particular node to be located easily given the value of its Data field. It is usually much faster to search a tree structure than to search an array containing the equivalent data elements — this is especially true when the number of elements becomes large. The Find() function is recursive and resembles the Add() function:

```
NODE* NODE::Find(int data) {
  if (data == Data)
    return this;
  if (data<Data && Left)
    return Left->Find(data);
  else if (data>Data && Right)
    return Right->Find(data);
  return 0;
}
```

The tree is searched by invoking the Find() function on the root node:

```
NODE* node = root->Find(2);
```

By providing each node with a key-value pair as data, the tree could be used to implement a dictionary — see section 8.6 for more details.

11.6 Heaps

A heap is closely related to a tree — the main difference is that a heap reorganises itself so that recently added nodes appear near the root. Heaps are commonly employed to manage storage space since the rapid location of frequently-used storage improves efficiency. The BLOCK class will implement a heap data structure — for a memory management application new BLOCK objects can be allocated using a similar technique to that described in section 10.4 for the POOL class.

The BLOCK **class has the following specification:**

```
class BLOCK {
public:
  BLOCK(int);
  void Add(BLOCK*&);
  void Remove(BLOCK*&);
    .
    .
private:
  BLOCK* Left;
  BLOCK* Right;
  BLOCK* Parent;
  int Data;
};
```

The constructor zeroes the pointer fields and sets the Data field using the parameter passed in. The Add() function has the following recursive definition:

```
void BLOCK::Add(BLOCK*& root) {
  if (!root)
    Left = Right = 0;
  else if (Data < root->Data) {
    Add(root->Left);
    root->Left = Right;
    if (Right) Right->Parent = root;
    Right = root;
    root->Parent = this;
  }
  else {
    Add(root->Right);
    root->Right = Left;
    if (Left) Left->Parent = root;
    Left = root;
    root->Parent = this;
  }
  root = this;
  Parent = 0;
}
```

The following figures illustrates the transformations applied after the recursive calls to Add() — note that the nested calls leave the new node at the top of the sub-tree. During these transformations it is essential to maintain the ordering of tree nodes that was described in section 11.5 — this is achieved by ensuring that the relative positions of the nodes from left to right (as depicted below) are unaffected by the reorganisation of the heap.

Firstly, when the new node is inserted in the left sub-tree of the root:

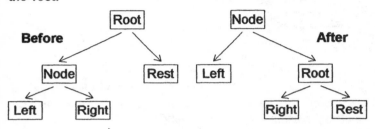

In this case the following two steps are performed:

1. Move the right sub-tree of the new node to the old root node as its left sub-tree

2. Move the old root (and its sub-trees) to the right sub-tree of the new node

Secondly, when the new node is inserted in the right sub-tree of the root:

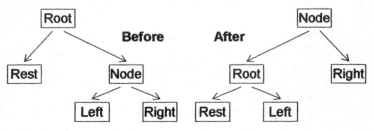

The two transformation steps are simliar to before but are reversed left-to-right. In any event, the new node always finishes at the top of the heap!

The Remove() function deletes just one block from the heap:

```
void BLOCK::Remove(BLOCK*& root) {
  BLOCK* block;
  if (!Right) block = Left;
  if (!Left) block = Right;
  if (Left && Right) {
    block = Left;
    while (block->Right)
      block = block->Right;
    block->Right = Right;
    Right->Parent = block;
    block = Left;
  }
  Left = Right = 0;
  if (block)
    block->Parent = Parent;
  if (!Parent)
    root = block;
  else if (Parent->Left == this)
    Parent->Left = block;
  else
    Parent->Right = block;
  Parent = 0;
}
```

If the removed node has only a left or right sub-tree, the root node in this sub-tree is used to replace its parent. Otherwise the right sub-tree is moved into the left sub-tree and the root of the left sub-tree replaces the removed node. For example:

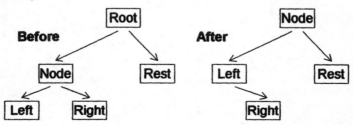

· **133**

Both the Add() and Remove() functions maintain the correct ordering of nodes within the heap and so the Find() function defined for trees in section 11.5 will work here too.

11.7 Collection Classes

Objects from the ITEM, NODE and BLOCK classes are able to assemble themselves into list, tree and heap data structures. The implementation of the functionality is hidden within these classes — this is a good example of the object oriented approach. However, it may be useful to process the collection of objects within each hierarchical data structure as a whole — this is the purpose of collection classes such as LIST, TREE and HEAP. These classes provide higher level services that may build on the functionality of the ITEM, NODE and BLOCK classes. For example, the LIST class could perform services such as the following:

1. Manage the list's header object
2. Track the current length of the list
3. Generate a new ITEM object and then call the object's Add() function to place it at the head of the list

The third option is made available by defining an Insert() function for the LIST class — the service is requested by invoking the function.

The essential idea is to separate the low-level code for manipulating the individual data elements from the high-level services which treat the collection of elements as a single data structure.

12. Templates

C++ templates provide an important mechanism for creating reusable software. The data processing performed by C++ functions and classes is often influenced by the parameter values supplied to them — these parameters can be variables of basic and structured data types or even objects of user-defined classes. Templates extend the notion of parameterization by permitting not only data values to be parameterized but also data types. C++ template classes enable the parameterization of data types by treating a single template class as a blue-print for a whole collection of classes — each of the classes generated from the template performs essentially the same processing but acts on variables and objects of differing types. Consequently, the software which defines a template class may be reused many times and unnecessary duplication of coding effort can be avoided.

12.1 Type Parameters

The behaviour of an object can be controlled by passing various parameters to its constructor. For example, the ARRAY class of section 9.3 checks subscript values against the bounds of an array — depending on the parameters passed to the constructor of an ARRAY object, the upper and lower bounds of the associated array change. Hence one ARRAY object may accept a particular subscript whilst another will reject it — the ARRAY class parameterizes the array bounds. However, the data type of the array elements is the same (`float`) for all ARRAY objects. To handle bounds checking for an array of a new data type it would be necessary to duplicate all the code for the ARRAY class and then make the appropriate changes by replacing type `float` with the new data type. An alternative approach that avoids the duplication of code is to parameterize the data type of the array elements — C++ templates are designed to accommodate type parameterizations.

12.2 Template Classes

A template class may parameterize a data type — the template serves as a blue-print for a whole collection of C++ classes all of which perform essentially the same processing but applied to variables and objects of different data types. For example, the ARRAY class may be converted into a template as follows:

```
template <class T>
class ARRAY {
public:
  T& operator[](int);
   .
   .
private:
  T Array[100];
};
```

A C++ template is prefixed by the **template** keyword and a list of the template parameters in angle brackets. The parameters can accept constant values (such as integers) but a more common application is to parameterize a data type — the keyword **class** is used to indicate a type parameter and the parameterized type name follows.

For the parameterized version of the ARRAY class, the Array field is an array of one hundred elements of data type T and the overloaded subscript operator returns a reference to one of these elements.

The **template** keyword is also required when the template class is defined:

```
template <class T>
T& ARRAY<T>::operator[] (int i) {
   .
   .
   // define function here
   .
   .
}
```

Function definitions for a template class should accompany the class specification in the header file. The name of the template class is ARRAY<T> — when a concrete class is generated from a class template the actual type name replaces the T parameter in the class name.

It is now easy to create an ARRAY object which performs bounds checking on an integer array with ten elements — all that is required is the following declaration statement:

```
ARRAY<int> x(10);
```

The compiler takes care of generating the class code for this choice of type parameter. Only code that is actually used will be generated — to force the compiler to provide all the code for the ARRAY<int> class the following statement may be used:

```
template ARRAY<int>;
```

12.3 The VECTOR Class

The VECTOR class provides a fuller example of working with C++ class templates. Each VECTOR object represents a vector with components (x,y,z) in three-dimensional space — the VECTOR class is useful for solving problems in cartesian geometry or linear algebra. The class provides overloaded operators to calculate the scalar and vector products of a pair of vectors. For two vectors $a==(x,y,z)$ and $b==(X,Y,Z)$ the scalar product is:

$$a|b == x*X + y*Y + z*Z$$

and the vector product is:

$$a*b == (y*Z-z*Y, z*X-x*Z, x*Y-y*X)$$

These operations can be used to calculate the determinant of a matrix M composed of the three vectors a, b and c:

$$det(M) == a|(b*c) == c|(a*b) == b|(c*a)$$

The VECTOR class is parameterized so that it will work with floating-point or integer component values — the latter choice can provide faster computations.

137

The VECTOR class specification follows:

```
template <class T>
class VECTOR {
public:
   VECTOR(T = 0,T = 0,T = 0);
   T operator|(const VECTOR<T>&) const;
   VECTOR<T> operator*(const VECTOR<T>&) const;

      .
      .
private:
   T X,Y,Z;
};
```

In a real implementation the class should be made regular (see chapter 8) — the addition and subtraction operators could also be usefully overloaded. The details are omitted here so that the essentials of defining a template class can be emphasized.

The constructor sets the X, Y and Z fields from the arguments supplied:

```
   template <class T>
   VECTOR<T>::VECTOR(T x,T y,T z) {
      X = x;
      Y = y;
      Z = z;
   }
```

Note that the <T> extension to the class name need not be applied to the constructor in either the class specification or the function definition — the same is true for the destructor.

The scalar product is calculated with the following function:

```
template <class T>
T
VECTOR<T>::operator|(const VECTOR<T>& v) const
{
   return X*v.X+Y*v.Y+Z*v.Z;
}
```

The vector product is constructed with a local VECTOR<T> object:

```
template <class T>
VECTOR<T>
VECTOR<T>::operator* (const VECTOR<T>& v) const
    VECTOR<T> product;
    product.X = Y*v.Z-Z*v.Y;
    product.Y = Z*v.X-X*v.Z;
    product.Z = X*v.Y-Y*v.X;
    return product;
}
```

The following code calculates a determinant value:

```
VECTOR<int> a(9,5,3);
VECTOR<int> b(4,1,7);
VECTOR<int> c(6,8,2);
int det = a|(b*c);
```

Such a calculation is useful when solving simultaneous linear equations in three unknowns x, y and z.

12.4 Wrapper Classes

Template classes can help to avoid the duplication of source code. However, there is a problem — the object code for each of the classes built from a template must still be generated whenever it is required. This automatic generation of object code can increase the size of an executable file considerably. The effect may be lessened by placing most of the implementation in a concrete class and then wrapping this class with a template class — in this case only the wrapper code is duplicated and such code can be kept to a minimum. The concrete class typically operates with void pointers so that it can handle any type of data and the wrapper classes provide type checking.

To provide an example of wrapper classes, the LIST class is defined here as a collection class for the ITEM objects of section 11.3 — objects of the ITEM class store their data using a void pointer. The template class BASKET acts as a

139

wrapper that performs compile-time type checking on the items stored by the `LIST` class — it also casts `void` pointers to the appropriate type when items are retrieved from the list. The `SetData()` and `GetData()` functions for the `ITEM` class are defined below:

```
void ITEM::SetData(void* data) {
  Data = data;
}

void* ITEM::GetData(void) {
  return Data;
}
```

The `Shift()` function allows the `LIST` class to move along its list of `ITEM` objects:

```
ITEM* ITEM::Shift(void) {
  return Next;
}
```

The function could be parameterized to permit shifts in both directions.

The `LIST` class has the following specification:

```
class LIST {
public:
  LIST(void);
  ~LIST(void);
  void Insert(void*);
  void* Extract(void);
    .
    .
private:
  ITEM* Header;
  int Length;
};
```

Most of the functionality for processing the list data structure is placed in the `LIST` class — the code for the corresponding wrapper class is kept to a minimum.

The LIST constructor creates a header item:

```
LIST::LIST(void) {
  Header = (ITEM*) new ITEM;
  Length = 0;
}
```

and the destructor empties the list:

```
LIST::~LIST(void) {
  ITEM* item;
  while (Length--) {
    item = Header->Shift();
    item->Remove();
    delete item;
  }
  delete Header;
}
```

The Insert() function creates a new ITEM object, sets its data and calls its Add() function to place it at the head of the list:

```
void LIST::Insert(void* data) {
  ITEM* item = (ITEM*) new ITEM;
  item->SetData(data);
  item->Add(Header);
  Length++;
}
```

The Extract() function similarly retrieves data from the head of the list:

```
void* LIST::Extract(void) {
  if (!Length) return 0;
  ITEM* item = Header->Shift();
  void* data = item->GetData();
  item->Remove();
  delete item;
  Length--;
  return data;
}
```

Now a template wrapper class is straightforward to define
— the BASKET class specification is:

```
template <class T>
class BASKET {
public:
  BASKET(void);
  ~BASKET(void);
  void Store(T);
  T Retrieve(void);
private:
  LIST* List;
};
```

The BASKET class constructor and destructor simply create
and destroy the associated LIST object. The Store()
function is:

```
template <class T>
void BASKET<T>::Store(T data) {
  T* pointer = (T*) new T;
  *pointer = data;
  List->Insert(pointer);
}
```

A dynamic object of the parameterized type is created and
its value is set using the argument passed to the Store()
function — note that this assumes there is an appropriate
assignment operator available. Since the Store() function
accepts data of a definite type, the compiler can perform
type-checking on the data that is to be inserted into the list.
The Retrieve() function is defined as follows:

```
template <class T>
T BASKET<T>::Retrieve(void) {
  T* pointer = (T*) List->Extract();
  if (!pointer) return 0;
  T data = *pointer;
  delete pointer;
  return data;
}
```

Note that the `void` pointer returned by the LIST object is cast to point at data of the parameterized type — the referenced data is saved in a local variable before the dynamic object that stored it is destroyed.

The BASKET class is a fairly general class for storing and retrieving objects — it need not use a LIST object to provide its implementation. For example, the BASKET class specification may be modified to include a second parameterized type:

```
template <class V,class T>
class BASKET {
      .
      .
private:
   V* Holder;
};
```

The references to List in the Store() and Retrieve() functions should be updated to refer instead to Holder. Then any holder type V which supplies suitable Insert() and Extract() functions can be used with the BASKET template class. The HEAP class might be one possibility:

```
BASKET<HEAP,int> basket;
basket.Store(6);
```

This code stores the integer value 6 in a wrapped HEAP structure.

12.5 Template Functions

The C++ template mechanism also works with global functions — every template parameter should appear in the specification for the function parameter list. For example, a template function Debug() may be defined that prints debugging information about any variable or object it receives as a parameter:

```
template <class T> void Debug(const T&);
```

A template function is defined in the usual way but the
template keyword and the template parameter list must
precede the definition:

```
template <class T>
void Debug(const T& object) {
    cout << "Object at address: ";
    cout << hex << &object << dec;
    cout << '\n';
}
```

This function prints out the location in memory of its
object parameter. The stream manipulator `hex` changes
the format in which the address is displayed to hexadecimal
— similarly `dec` changes the format back to decimal.

A non-template version of `Debug()` which explicitly
specifies a parameter type will override the template
function for that type. For example:

```
void Debug(const int& i) {
    cout << "Integer (" << i;
    cout << ") at address: ";
    cout << hex << &i << dec;
    cout << '\n';
}
```

The following code:

```
OBJECT object;
int i(0);
Debug(object);
Debug(i);
```

prints the debugging information:

```
Object at address: 0x4153e57c
Integer (0) at address: 0x4153e578
```

As with template classes the object code for template
functions is only generated by the compiler whenever it is
required.

13. Inheritance

Inheritance is the principal mechanism in C++ for enabling polymorphism — a collection of objects are polymorphic if they exhibit different behaviours from one another when they are sent identical messages. Encapsulation and polymorphism form the foundations of the object oriented programming philosophy — encapsulation is concerned with hiding implementation details whilst polymorphism allows diverse functionality to be exposed to the outside world through a well-defined communications interface. One C++ class may derive some of its characteristics from another by the process of inheritance. In particular, each derived class inherits the interface defined by its base class — when new implementations are provided for each derived class objects from different derived classes become polymorphic. This chapter covers the details of C++ inheritance — topics include the specification of base and derived classes, the process of inheriting or overriding base class fields and functions, the invocation of real and virtual functions, and finally the construction and destruction procedures for objects of derived classes.

13.1 Base and Derived Classes

In C++ one class may be derived from another — the original class is known as the base class of the derived class. The derived class inherits many of its characteristics from the base class — these fall into three categories:

1. Data
2. Code
3. Interfaces

The first two are the subject of this chapter whilst chapter 14 deals with interfaces. The data fields defined by the base class are present in all objects of the derived class — the derived class may add more data fields if it needs them. Similarly, the functions of the base class are inherited by objects of the derived class — the exceptions to this rule include the base class constructor and destructor as well as any overloaded assignment operators provided by the base class. In particular, the inheritance of class characteristics applies to static fields and functions — however, the static data fields for base and derived classes are distinct.

Any C++ class can act as a base class but a good base class is specifically designed as such. A base class should ideally contain only functionality that is sufficiently general to make the base class widely applicable — at the very least it should be possible to derive at least two distinct classes from a base class. In other words C++ inheritance is a mechanism for software reuse — the source code provided by the base class need not be duplicated for each of the derived classes.

13.2 Deriving a Class

The derivation of a new class from a base class is straightforward. The following specification for the DERIVED class states that it inherits from the BASE class:

```
class DERIVED : public BASE {
    .
    .
};
```

The derived class name is followed by the : symbol, then the keyword **public** and finally the base class name. The **public** keyword indicates that the derivation is public — this is the commonest sort of inheritance. In fact, public derivation is the only kind of inheritance described in this book and the **public** keyword may be omitted. The class specification for the DERIVED class must occur after the BASE class specification — a typical approach is to include a header file for the BASE class.

In general, the DERIVED class can use its inherited fields and functions exactly as if it had defined them itself. For example, suppose the BASE class has a Data field and

146

also a `Print()` function:

```
class BASE {
public:
   void Print(void);
   int Data;
};
```

The `DERIVED` class can create objects just like any other class:

```
DERIVED object;
```

and such objects inherit their characteristics from the `BASE` class:

```
object.Data = 0;
object.Print();
```

However, base class pointers can reference objects of the derived class — indeed, a pointer to the derived class will be implicitly cast to a base class pointer when required. For example:

```
DERIVED object;
BASE* pointer = &object;
```

Here there is an implicit cast from `DERIVED*` pointer type to `BASE*` pointer type before the `pointer` variable receives the address of the object. This situation is similar to that with `void` pointers — any type of data may be referenced by a `void` pointer and implicit casts to `void*` pointer type are applied when necessary.

Casts in the opposite direction from base class pointers to derived class pointers must be explicitly requested — the cast is only sensible when the referenced object is known to belong to the derived class:

```
DERIVED object;
BASE* base = &object;
DERIVED* derived = (DERIVED*) base;
```

147

Finally, the DERIVED class may itself act as a base class for yet another derived class. All the fields and functions of the DERIVED class (including those inherited from the BASE class) are available for inheriting as part of the new base class. In this way an extended chain of classes can be built with each class inheriting from the previous one in the chain.

13.3 Protection Keywords

The private, protected and public keywords guard against improper use of class fields and functions. The private and public keywords have appeared in many classes in previous chapters — the protected keyword is only relevant when inheritance is involved. The public keyword allows any source code to reference a field or invoke a function — the private keyword restricts these activities to functions belonging to the class and friend functions. The private and public keywords provide control that is too coarse when inheritance is involved. A derived class may need fields or functions from the base class — the private keyword is too restrictive but the public keyword releases all control. In these situations the protected keyword should appear in the base class specification before any fields and functions that a derived class may need — protected fields and functions can be used by both the base and derived class functions as well as friends of these classes. With public derivation the protected members of the base class become protected members of the derived class — this is useful if the derived class becomes the base class for yet another derived class.

Finally, note that the private, protected and public keywords only provide compile-time protection — they are intended to identify inadvertent uses of fields and functions. It is easy to by-pass these protection mechanisms at run-time using devious means — for example, an object pointer may be cast to a character pointer and the entire contents of the object read byte by byte.

13.4 Field and Function Overriding

Derived classes may define new fields in addition to those they inherit from their base class. For example:

```
class BASE {
protected:
  int Data;
    .
    .
};

class DERIVED : public BASE {
private:
  int Array[100];
    .
    .
};
```

Here the base class has the integer `Data` field — this is inherited by the `DERIVED` class which also defines a new `Array` field. If the same name is used for fields in both the base and derived classes then the latter field overrides the former — within the functions of the derived class the name refers to the derived class field. For example:

```
class DERIVED : public BASE {
public:
  void SetData(float);
private:
  float Data;
    .
    .
};

void DERIVED::SetData(float data) {
  Data = data;
}
```

Here the `SetData()` function assigns a value to the floating-point field of the `DERIVED` class and not the integer field inherited from the `BASE` class. To reference the overridden field the `::` operator is available. For example:

```
class DERIVED : public BASE {
public:
  void SetData(float);
  void SetData(int);
private:
  float Data;
    .
    .
};

void DERIVED::SetData(float data) {
  Data = data;
}

void DERIVED::SetData(int data) {
  BASE::Data = data;
}
```

The `SetData()` function is overloaded to permit either base or derived field to be set.

An alternative approach is have a `SetData()` function defined in both base and derived classes — the base class function is overridden much like the base class `Data` field was overridden previously. However, a derived class function overrides all functions with the same name that occur in the base class — overloading the base class functions with different parameter lists does not prevent the overriding. The new BASE class specification is:

```
class BASE {
public:
  void SetData(int);
    .
    .
private:
  int Data;
};
```

The BASE class defines a `SetData()` function which

accepts an integer parameter:

```
void BASE::SetData(int data) {
  Data = data;
}
```

The `DERIVED` class has a `SetData()` function that overrides the `BASE` class version even though it accepts a different parameter type:

```
class DERIVED : public BASE {
public:
  DERIVED(void);
  void SetData(float);

    .
    .
private:
  float Data;
};

void DERIVED::SetData(float data) {
  Data = data;
}
```

The `DERIVED` class constructor zeroes both the `Data` fields with function calls:

```
DERIVED::DERIVED(void) {
  SetData(0);
  BASE::SetData(0);
}
```

The first function call to `SetData()` invokes the `DERIVED` class function — the overridden base class version must be invoked using the `::` operator.

13.5 Virtual Functions

The previous section described the overriding of class functions — the functions there were real functions but C++ also supports virtual functions. Virtual functions behave somewhat differently to real functions — they are only important when dealing with objects of a derived class. Virtual functions are marked as such by preceding them in the class specfication with the `virtual` keyword. As an example of virtual functions the FRUIT base class will be defined:

```
class FRUIT {
public:
  void WhoAmI(void) const;
protected:
  virtual void GetName(void) const;
};
```

The `WhoAmI()` function is invoked to tell a FRUIT to print a description of itself:

```
void FRUIT::WhoAmI(void) const {
  cout << "I am ";
  GetName();
}
```

The `GetName()` function actually supplies the name of the fruit — the FRUIT class is a base class and represents all fruits so its `GetName()` function is general:

```
void FRUIT::GetName(void) const {
  cout << "a fruit.\n";
}
```

The following code:

```
FRUIT fruit;
fruit.WhoAmI();
```

prints the message:

```
I am a fruit.
```

Now that the FRUIT base class has been defined specific fruit classes can be derived from it — the derived classes will print a particular fruit name when the `WhoAmI()`

function is invoked. For example, the `APPLE` fruit class follows:

```
class APPLE : public FRUIT {
protected:
  virtual void GetName(void) const;
};

void APPLE::GetName(void) const {
  cout << "an apple.\n";
}
```

The `APPLE` class inherits the `WhoAmI()` function and overrides the `GetName()` function. An `APPLE` object may be created and the `WhoAmI()` function invoked:

```
APPLE apple;
apple.WhoAmI();
```

This executes the code for the `WhoAmI()` code from the `FRUIT` base class. If the `GetName()` function were real the result would be:

```
I am a fruit.
```

However, the following situation now arises:

1. A base class function executes within an object of a derived class
2. The base class function invokes a virtual function
3. The derived class of the object overrides the virtual function

In these circumstances the base class function must call the derived class version of the virtual function.

Here the base class function is `WhoAmI()`, the object is `apple` and it belongs to the derived `APPLE` class which overrides the virtual `GetName()` function. Hence the `WhoAmI()` function must use the `APPLE` class version of the `GetName()` function.

The `apple.WhoAmI()` call thus produces the message:

```
I am an apple.
```

When the `WhoAmI()` function is invoked for objects of different classes (`FRUIT` or `APPLE`) the processing that is performed differs — this is an example of polymorphism. The next section provides another example and Chapter 14 discusses the whole subject in more detail.

13.6 Pointers and Functions

The previous two sections have discussed the selection of a real or virtual function when the function invocation is made directly by name. Actually, these function calls employ the implicit `this` pointer — this section extends the ideas to cover function invocations made through a general pointer. For real functions the decision of whether to call the base class function or an overriding version from a derived class is made at compile-time. If the function is invoked using a base class pointer then the base class function is used — this is true even if the base class pointer references an object of a derived class. To provide an example the following modifications are made to the `FRUIT` class:

```
class FRUIT {
public:
  void WhoAmI(void) const;
};

void FRUIT::WhoAmI(void) const {
  cout << "I am a fruit.\n";
}
```

and to the derived `APPLE` class:

```
class APPLE : public FRUIT{
public:
  void WhoAmI(void) const;
};

void APPLE::WhoAmI(void) const {
  cout << "I am an apple.\n";
}
```

The code below demonstrates the choice of real function:

```
FRUIT* fruit = (FRUIT*) new FRUIT;
FRUIT* apple = (FRUIT*) new APPLE;
fruit->WhoAmI();
apple->WhoAmI();
```

Both calls to WhoAmI() print the message:

```
I am a fruit.
```

To obtain the proper response from the apple object it is necessary to cast its pointer to APPLE* type. For example:

```
APPLE* apple = (APPLE*) new APPLE;
apple->WhoAmI();
```

Now the derived class function is invoked. In general, to obtain the overriding version of a real function, a derived object must be referenced by a pointer for the derived class.

These rules also cover function invocations made through the implicit **this** pointer. Within base class functions the **this** pointer is a base class pointer whilst within functions explicitly defined by the derived class the **this** pointer is a derived class pointer — however, within functions inherited from the base class the **this** pointer is a base class pointer.

The choice of virtual functions is not made at compile time but at run-time and the class of the object is important as well as the pointers used. For a base class object, the base class virtual function is invoked — similarly for a derived class object referenced through a pointer for the derived class, the derived class virtual function is invoked. The interesting case occurs when:

1. A base class pointer references an object of the derived class

2. The pointer is used to invoke a virtual function

3. The derived class of the object overrides the virtual function

This situation exactly mirrors that involving the implicit `this` pointer as discussed at the end in section 13.5. Consequently, the derived class version of the virtual function is invoked. As an example, the APPLE and BANANA classes are both derived from the FRUIT base class and this class now adds the keyword `virtual` to its WhoAmI() function to make it virtual:

```
class FRUIT {
public:
   virtual void WhoAmI() const;
};

class APPLE : public FRUIT {
public:
   virtual void WhoAmI() const;
};

class BANANA : public FRUIT
public:
   virtual void WhoAmI() const;
};
```

The overriding versions of the WhoAmI() function are suitably defined. The following code processes a BASKET object (see section 12.4) which holds a collection of FRUIT* pointers:

```
BASKET<FRUIT*> basket;
FRUIT* apple = (FRUIT*) new APPLE;
FRUIT* banana = (FRUIT*) new BANANA;
basket.Store(apple);
basket.Store(banana);
FRUIT* fruit;
while (fruit = basket.Retrieve()) {
   fruit->WhoAmI();
   delete fruit;
}.
```

When the WhoAmI() function is called for each of the fruits in the basket, the appropriate derived class version of the virtual function is chosen. If a first-in-last-out storage mechanism for the `basket` object is assumed then the code prints the following:

```
I am a banana.
I am an apple.
```

This is another example of polymorphism — the `APPLE` and `BANANA` objects perform different processing when the `WhoAmI()` function is invoked.

There is an exception to the above rules for function selection. When a base class constructor (or destructor) is called during the creation (or destruction) of a derived class object the implicit `this` pointer is a base class pointer — however, only functions from the base class are invoked even if they are virtual and overridden by the derived class. The following sections discuss the construction and destruction processes more fully.

13.7 Derived Class Constructors

The standard procedure for creating and destroying an object was discussed in chapter 7 — there are a number of modifications when the object belongs to a derived class. At creation the following steps are taken:

1. Storage Allocation
2. Base Class Initialization
3. Derived Class Initialization

The base class initialization step intializes any objects embedded by the base class and then invokes the base class constructor code. The base class initialization is not influenced by the existence of the derived class — in particular no virtual functions from the derived class are invoked. The derived class initialization performs similar processing for the derived class — the fields and functions inherited from the base class are available at this point.

Chapter 7 introduced the : notation for choosing a constructor for any embedded objects — this notation may also indicate which constructor will initialize the base class. If no constructor is explicitly specified for an embedded object or the base class then the default constructor of the appropriate class is invoked. For example, the EMBEDDED class holds a string passed to its constructor:

```
class EMBEDDED {
public:
  EMBEDDED(const char*);
    .
    .
private:
  char String[100];
  int Length;
};
EMBEDDED::EMBEDDED(const char* string) {
  Length = 0;
  if (!string) return;
  while (String[Length] = *string++)
    Length++;
}
```

The BASE class uses an embedded object to hold a "Base" string in its BaseName field:

```
class BASE {
public:
  BASE(int = 0);
    .
    .
private:
  EMBEDDED BaseName;
};
BASE::BASE(int i) : BaseName("Base") {
    .
    .
}
```

As described in section 7.6 the embedded BaseName object is initialized just before the BASE class constructor is executed.

Now the DERIVED class is derived from the BASE class — it also embeds an EMBEDDED object but passes a "Derived" string instead of a "Base" string as a parameter:

```
class DERIVED : public BASE {
public:
  DERIVED(void);
    .
    .
private:
  EMBEDDED Name;
};

DERIVED::DERIVED(void)
  : BASE(123), Name("Derived") {
    .
    .
}
```

In fact, a DERIVED object contains two EMBEDDED objects — one inherited from the BASE class and another embedded directly. As well as initializing the second of these objects, the DERIVED class constructor explicitly passes the value 123 to the BASE class constructor.

13.8 Virtual Destructors

The destruction process is the exact opposite of the creation process:

1. Derived Class Finalization
2. Base Class Finalization
3. Storage Deallocation

The derived class finalization invokes the derived class destructor and then finalizes any objects embedded by the derived class. The base class finalization performs simliar processing for the base class. However, when a derived class object has the **delete** operator applied to a base class pointer which references it, the derived class finalization is not performed if the destructors are real functions. To avoid this happening the destructors should be

159

declared as virtual functions:

```
class BASE {
public:
  virtual ~BASE(void);
    .
    .
};

class DERIVED: public BASE {
public:
  virtual ~DERIVED(void);
    .
    .
};
```

Furthermore, if the derived class overloads the `delete` operator its version is only invoked if the destructors are virtual. Alternatively, if the derived class inherits an overloaded `delete` operator from the base class which has two parameters, then the second parameter (of `size_t` type) will only report the correct size for derived objects if virtual destructors are used.

14. Interfaces

An interface class contains no code — its sole purpose is to force a derived class to support a well-defined set of functions. Interface classes are abstract classes and cannot generate objects directly — derived classes must provide implementations of the interface's functions before objects can be created. Objects from different classes that implement the same interface are interchangeable with one another — this is a classic example of polymorphism. A notification class is a type of interface class that allows an object to send notifications of internal events — notifications complete the two-way exchange of messages between objects. Within a software component an object typically supports multiple interfaces each representing a different facet of the object's functionality. The UNKNOWN interface class is designed to simplify the use of multiple interfaces with C++ objects — smart pointers can automate some of the troublesome book-keeping details.

14.1 Pure Virtual Functions

The previous chapter introduced the notion of virtual functions — the FRUIT base class contained general implementations of its virtual functions which where overridden by more specific implementations in the derived classes. However, it is possible to declare a virtual function in a base class without providing any implementation of the function — such a function is known as a pure virtual function and it is denoted in the base class specification with the =0 marker. For example:

```
class FRUIT {
public:
  virtual void Draw(void) = 0;
    .
    .
};
```

Here the FRUIT class defines a pure virtual Draw() function — the function draws an illustration of the fruit represented by an object. Without a generic depiction of a fruit the Draw() function cannot be implemented in the base class — instead it must be overridden in each derived class by providing code that draws individual fruits.

If a class defines a pure virtual function or inherits such a function without overiding it then the class is an abstract class. An abstract class cannot be used to create objects — however, a class derived from the abstract class which implements all its virtual functions can create objects. Consequently the pure virtual functions declared by a base class force the derived classes to support these functions as part of their communications interface — for example, every object of a class derived from the FRUIT class can be sent a message by invoking its Draw() function.

An extreme example of this approach is to specify a base class which contains only pure virtual functions — the class is then known as an interface class. If a concrete class inherits its interface from such a class, there is complete separation of interface and implementation. For example:

```
class HOLDER {
public:
  virtual void Insert(int) = 0;
  virtual int Extract(void) = 0;
};
```

The HOLDER interface class specifies an interface that must be supported by all classes derived it. The interface defines the services which may be expected from a class designed to hold a collection of integer values — the LIST, TREE and HEAP collection classes discussed in section 11.7 are examples of classes that could support the HOLDER interface.

14.2 Polymorphism

In a C++ context polymorphism occurs when a collection of objects each exhibit their own individual behaviours upon receipt of identical messages — the name polymorphism is applied because the objects in the collection represent many possible forms. Polymorphism arises when interface and implementation are separated — the interface remains constant but the implementation may change. The following figure illustrates the process of communicating with an object through an interface defined by an interface class:

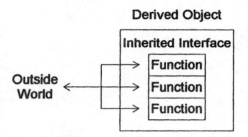

Derived Object

As long as the functions in the interface remain the same the underlying object may be changed — any object which supports the same interface will suffice. Of course, for this to work it is necessary to define the processing expected of each interface function — the interface class only fixes the function parameter formats and the function return types. It is the responsibility of the implementor of a new class supporting the interface to adhere to the functionality specification. The interchangeability of objects that results when a number of classes are derived from a common interface is a classic example of polymorphism — objects of different derived types are sent the same messages through the inherited interface but perform their own individual processing.

In general, an interface is used to group together a related set of functions and hence it defines one facet of an object's functionality. The C++ language only allows an object to support one interface directly — section 14.4 discusses techniques for overcoming this limitation. Nonetheless, an object may conceptually support any number of interfaces — each interface is specified by a different interface class.

The following figure depicts an object with two distinct interfaces:

Object with Multiple Interfaces

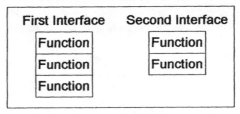

To permit one object to be substituted for another they must both support a common set of interfaces — the individual objects are polymorphic with respect to this shared set of interfaces. Of course, the two objects may also support other interfaces which they do not share but the polymorphism does not extend to these interfaces.

14.3 Notification Classes

Notification classes are a useful variety of interface class. These classes are needed when an object wishes to notify the outside world of events that occur within the object — they complement other interface classes which permit messages to be sent to an object from the outside world. The following figure demonstrates the idea:

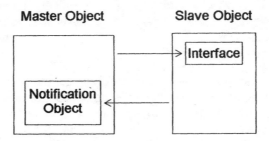

The master object sends messages to the slave through the usual interface communications mechanism — if the slave wants to send messages back to the master it passes them to a notification object within the master. The slave class catalogues the sorts of messages it will send by defining an associated notification class — this is an interface base class from which the actual class of the notification object must be derived.

The notification class NOTIFY specifies an interface with two functions:

```
class NOTIFY {
public:
  virtual void MultipleEvents(int) = 0;
  virtual void SingleEvent(void) = 0;
  const static int Event_1;
  const static int Event_2;
};
```

The notification class is designed to provide notification of three possible events that may occur within a SLAVE object: FirstEvent, SecondEvent and ThirdEvent. The function MultipleEvents() is called if either of the first two events occurs whilst the SingleEvent() function is only called if the last event occurs. The function MultipleEvents() passes one of the constants Event_1 or Event_2 as a parameter to identify the relevant event. Constant static data fields are acceptable additions to an interface class — they should be defined globally:

```
const int NOTIFY::Event_1 = 1;
const int NOTIFY::Event_2 = 2;
```

The SLAVE class source file is a good place for these constant definitions.

Whenever a MASTER object wants to receive notifications from a SLAVE object it must derive its own class from the NOTIFY class.

For example:

```
class MONITOR : public NOTIFY {
public:
  virtual void MultipleEvents(int);
  virtual void SingleEvent(void);
};
```

The interface functions are provided with appropriate implementations:

```
void MONITOR::MultipleEvents(int event) {
  if (event == NOTIFY::Event_1) {
    // processing for FirstEvent
  }
  else if (event == NOTIFY::Event_2) {
    // processing for SecondEvent
  }
}

void MONITOR::SingleEvent(void) {
  // processing for ThirdEvent
}
```

The SLAVE object must be able to send messages to its master's notification object — a common technique is to pass a pointer into the SLAVE class constructor:

```
class SLAVE {
public:
  SLAVE(NOTIFY*);
  .
  .
private:
  NOTIFY* Notify;
};

SLAVE::SLAVE(NOTIFY* notify) {
  Notify = notify;
}
```

Now the MASTER object can create a SLAVE object and

pass it a pointer to the master's MONITOR object:

```
MONITOR monitor;
SLAVE slave(&monitor);
```

Since the MONITOR class is derived from the NOTIFY class the pointer is implicitly cast to NOTIFY* type. Now whenever an event occurs within the SLAVE object it can send a notification to the MASTER object:

```
      .
      .
if (Notify)
  Notify->MultipleEvents(NOTIFY::Event_1);
      .
      .
if (Notify)
  Notify->MultipleEvents(NOTIFY::Event_2);
      .
      .
if (Notify)
  Notify->SingleEvent();
      .
      .
```

The MultipleEvents() and SingleEvent() functions are invoked through a base pointer but they are virtual functions and so the code from the derived MONITOR class is executed. The MASTER object thus receives notifications from its SLAVE object.

14.4 The UNKNOWN Interface

Unfortunately the C++ language does not directly support the notion of objects with multiple interfaces. It does allow a derived class to inherit from multiple base classes through the mechanism of multiple inheritance but all the inherited functions are merged into a single interface. Provided the merging operation does not result in any function name clashes, the individual interfaces can be selected by appropriate pointer casting. Nonetheless, programming with multiple inheritance can rapidly become complicated and there is a simpler solution — the UNKNOWN interface. The UNKNOWN interface specifies the minimal functionality that any interface should provide in order to support objects with multiple interfaces — it forms a base class for all other such interfaces. The UNKNOWN class specification follows:

```
class UNKNOWN {
public:
  virtual int Query(int,UNKNOWN**) = 0;
  virtual void Acquire(void) = 0;
  virtual void Release(void) = 0;
};
```

The Query() function is the most important — its purpose is to determine which other interfaces an object supports. The first parameter provides an interface ID that uniquely identifies the type of interface required. If such an interface is supported by the object the function returns true and a pointer to the interface is stored at the address provided by the second parameter — otherwise the function returns false and a null pointer is stored. For example:

```
UNKNOWN* pointer = GetInterfacePointer(...);
UNKNOWN* interface;
int okay =
  pointer->Query(INTERFACE_ID,&interface);
```

The Query() call asks whether the object supports the interface identified by the INTERFACE_ID parameter — if it does the interface pointer is set to reference this interface. In this way any number of interface pointers can be acquired for the object's interfaces — however, the first one must be obtained in some other manner. A typical approach is to call an operating system function such as GetInterfacePointer() — the next section discusses this point in more detail.

Finally, an object should continue to exist as long as any pointers still reference its interfaces — when the last reference is removed the object can destroy itself. This mode of operation is enabled by the `Acquire()` and `Release()` functions which respectively increment and decrement a reference count held by the object — whenever a new interface pointer is returned by the `Query()` function the `Acquire()` function is called internally. Reference counting is discussed in more detail in section 10.3 — automating the calls to `Acquire()` and `Release()` is the subject of section 14.6.

14.5 Software Components

The UNKNOWN interface is particularly useful when working with software components. Each component registers the objects it contains and the interfaces supported by these objects. Code in other components can then call a function such as `GetInterfacePointer()` to request a particular interface pointer for a particular object. The register-request exchange to transfer interface pointers from one component to another must be mediated by the operating system — in Microsoft's model this is the responsibility of COM. The following figure demonstrates the process of exchanging an interface pointer:

Before Exchange

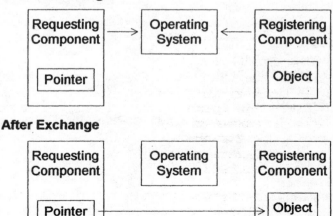

After Exchange

Once the interface pointer has been exchanged the operating system plays no further part and one component sends messages directly to an object in the other component. After the initial exchange further interface pointers for the object can be requested using the Query() function — the object may also provide other functions that return interface pointers to different objects within its component. A common technique is to arrange a component's objects within a hierarchy and let objects at each level supply pointers for objects at the next level — the first pointer requested is for an object at the top of the hierarchy.

14.6 Smart Interface Pointers

One problem with the Acquire() and Release() functions for interface pointers is that it is all too easy to forget to invoke them. Smart pointers can automate the process — see section 9.6 for more information. The approach adopted here uses the COMMON base class to provide the functionality common to all types of interface pointer — this base class is inherited by template classes that each correspond to a different interface type. The technique is similar to that described in section 12.4 but now inheritance replaces embedding as the wrapping mechanism. The COMMON class specification follows:

```
class COMMON {
public:
  COMMON(void);
  COMMON(int,int);
  COMMON(const COMMON&);
  ~COMMON(void);
  COMMON& operator=(const COMMON&);
  COMMON Query(int) const;
    .
    .
protected:
  UNKNOWN* Interface;
  int Status;
};
```

The default constructor simply sets the `Status` field to false. The next constructor is a wrapper function to invoke the `GetInterfacePointer()` function supplied by the operating system — it takes parameters to identify the type of object and interface required:

```
COMMON::COMMON(int classID,int interfaceID) {
   Status = GetInterfacePointer(classID,
         interfaceID,&Interface);
}
```

The copy constructor takes care of the call to `Acquire()` needed when an interface pointer is duplicated:

```
COMMON::COMMON(const COMMON& x) {
   Interface = x.Interface;
   Status = x.Status;
   if (Status)
      Interface->Acquire();
}
```

Similarly the destructor calls the `Release()` function:

```
COMMON::~COMMON(void) {
   if (Status)
      Interface->Release();
}
```

The assignment operator combines the actions of the destructor and copy constructor:

```
COMMON& COMMON::operator=(const COMMON& x) {
   if (this == &x)
      return *this;
   if (Status)
      Interface->Release();
   Interface = x.Interface;
   Status = x.Status;
   if (Status)
      Interface->Acquire();
   return *this;
}
```

The COMMON class `Query()` function is a wrapper function for the UNKNOWN interface `Query()` function:

```
COMMON COMMON::Query(int ID) const {
  COMMON x;
  if (Status) x.Status =
    Interface->Query(ID,&(x.Interface));
  return x;
}
```

The POINTER<T> template classes act as wrappers for the COMMON base class — the template class specification follows:

```
template <class T>
class POINTER : public COMMON {
public:
  POINTER(void);
  POINTER(int,int);
  POINTER(const COMMON&);
  POINTER<T>& operator=(const POINTER<T>&);
  T* operator->(void) const;
    .
    .
};
```

The three constructors just invoke their counterparts in the base class:

```
template <class T>
POINTER<T>::POINTER(void) : COMMON() {}
```

```
template <classT>
POINTER<T>::POINTER(int classID,
                              int interfaceID)
  : COMMON(classID,interfaceID) {}
```

```
template <class T>
POINTER<T>::POINTER(const COMMON& x)
  : COMMON(x) {}
```

The last of these acts as a type conversion operator — its

172

main purpose is to permit the result of a `Query()` request to be assigned to any type of POINTER<T> object.

Finally, the overloaded -> operator is used to invoke the other functions belonging to an interface — the template type parameter T is required so that the `Interface` pointer may be cast from UNKNOWN* type to T* type:

```
template <class T>
T* POINTER<T>::operator->(void) const {
  if (!Status)
    exit(999);
  return (T*)Interface;
}
```

The POINTER<T> template classes are easy to use — the `Acquire()` and `Release()` interface functions are invoked automatically whenever this is necessary. For example, suppose the INTERFACE class is derived from the UNKNOWN class and includes the `Explode()` function:

```
int main(void) {
  POINTER<UNKNOWN> first(CLASS_ID,UNKNOWN_ID);
  POINTER<INTERFACE> second;
  second = first.Query(INTERFACE_ID);
  second->Explode();
  return 0;
}
```

The CLASS_ID parameter selects a particular type of object whilst the UNKNOWN_ID and INTERFACE_ID parameters select the appropriate interfaces on the object. Note that the object is manipulated only through pointers to its interfaces and is never available directly. When the block statement of the `main()` function is exited, the `first` and `second` smart pointers are both destroyed — their destructors automatically release the interface pointers to the object. To hold an interface pointer from one block statement to another a dynamic POINTER<T> object may be used.

15. Exceptions

C++ exceptions provide a mechanism for structured error handling. Whenever an error is detected an exception may be thrown — this action passes information about the error from the point in the program where the error occurs to a higher level handler that knows how to deal with the problem. The C++ language defines the `try`, `throw` and `catch` keywords to support its exception mechanism — a section of code which may throw an exception is enclosed within a `try` block and thrown exceptions are caught by handlers that supply the error processing. In this way the program statements which perform the basic processing are separated from those which handle errors. The C++ exception mechanism is fully integrated with object creation and destruction procedures — whenever the throwing of an exception causes a block statement to be exited any local objects are automatically destroyed. Furthermore, an exception thrown from within an object constructor is treated in a unique manner.

15.1 Error Handling Schemes

The traditional approach to error handling is not structured — there are typically three options on finding an error:

1. Generate an error code
2. Transfer the flow of control
3. Terminate the program

An error code may be returned as the result of a function or used to set a global error variable. In either case the responsibility for handling the error is simply passed on — the error code should be tested at some point but this is not always done. For example, the `new` operator returns a null pointer if there is no more memory available to create a new object — the returned pointer should always be checked for a null value but this rarely happens.

The second option upon encountering an error is to transfer control to a set of program statements that will process the error — an error handler. This approach also requires constant checking for the occurrence of an error with the result that the main purpose of the code is often obscured. C++ provides the `goto` statement for transferring program control but the destination must be within the current function — the `setjmp()` and `longjmp()` functions provided by the standard C libraries can increase the extent of the jump but they do not interact well with C++ objects.

Finally, it may be impossible to handle an error satisfactorily and the only remaining option is to terminate the program — in earlier chapters the `exit()` function has been invoked when serious errors occur.

In many situations the processing of errors can be elegantly handled by the C++ exception mechanism. The technique combines the 'error code' and 'control transfer' approaches by passing error information directly from the point at which the error occurs to the error handler. This has several advantages:

1. Once an error is detected it cannot be overlooked
2. Most code can assume there are no errors
3. The error and its handler may be widely separated

The first statement holds since control is always transferred when an error is detected — furthermore, control will only flow normally if no errors are encountered so the second statement follows. Finally, errors usually occur within low-level routines which do not understand the context of the error sufficiently well to be able to handle them — this job is much better suited to higer level routines but these rarely bother to check for error codes generated by the functions they invoke. The exception mechanism can transfer information about the error directly from a low-level routine to its high-level handler.

176

15.2 Throwing Exceptions

An exception in C++ is a variable or object containing information about an error — it is transferred from the point at which the error occurs directly to an error handler. The process of reporting an error with an exception is known as throwing an exception — the `throw` keyword is used to throw an exception:

```
int error = 1001;
throw error;
```

Here the `throw` statement causes the integer error code 1001 to be passed to an error handler. For C++ to find a suitable handler the code must be enclosed in a `try` block:

```
try {
  .
  .
  int error = 1001;
  throw error;
  .
  .
}
catch (int i) {
  cout << "Error code " << i;
  cout << " caught.\n";
  exit(999);
}
```

The `try` block is followed by a `catch` block which contains the code for the error handler. In fact, any number of error handlers can follow a `try` block each with their own `catch` block — the different handlers are distinguished by the type of exception that they catch. The code within the `catch` blocks is only executed if an exception is thrown from the `try` block — if the `try` block is exited normally then control passes to the statement following the last `catch` block. The parentheses after the `catch` keyword contain the type of exception caught as well as the local name of the exception — an exception is always copied to a variable or object that is local to the catch block of the handler. The previous example copies the value of the `error` variable to the local variable `i` before printing the following message:

```
Error code 1001 caught.
```

The program then terminates with a call to the `exit()` function. When an error can be successfully handled the program may instead continue its execution — if a `catch` block completes normally control is transferred to the statement following the last `catch` block in the list.

The `INTEGER` class of chapter 9 is extended here to overload the division operator:

```
class MATH_ERROR {
public:
  int Code;
};

class INTEGER {
public:
  INTEGER(int = 0);
  INTEGER operator/(const INTEGER&) const;
  operator int(void) const;
    .
    .
private:
  int Data;
};
```

The overloaded / operator throws a `MATH_ERROR` exception if division by zero is attempted:

```
INTEGER
INTEGER::operator/(const INTEGER& i) const {
  if (i.Data == 0) {
    MATH_ERROR error;
    error.Code = 1001;
    throw error;
  }
  return INTEGER(Data/i.Data);
}
```

Now code may be written within a `try` block under the assumption that division by zero will not occur:

```
int i,j,k;
INTEGER I,J,K;
while (1) {
  try {
    cout << "Enter two integers ...\n";
    cin >> i >> j;
    I = INTEGER(i);
    J = INTEGER(j);
    K = I/J;
    k = int(K);
    cout << i << '/' << j;
    cout << " = " << k;
    cout << '\n';
  }
  catch (MATH_ERROR error) {
    if (error.Code == 1001)
      cout << "Division by Zero!\n";
  }
}
```

The `while` loop repeatedly asks for two integers and prints out the result of dividing one by the other. The actual division operator takes two INTEGER operands — there are type conversions from `int` to INTEGER and back. If the overloaded division operator from the INTEGER class detects an attempt to divide by zero a MATH_ERROR exception is thrown — the exception is caught by a handler and the following message is printed:

```
Division by Zero!
```

The `while` loop then continues to ask for another pair of integers. The important point to note is that the basic processing (input, division, ouput) can assume no errors will occur — the error handler is completely separate from the rest of the code.

15.3 Error Handler Selection

A `try` block may be followed by a number of `catch` blocks each for a different error handler — the question arises as to which handler to use when an exception is thrown. The previous section noted that a handler specifies which type of exception it catches by placing the type name in parentheses after the `catch` keyword — however, there are a few complications.

Firstly, the exception is always passed to the handler by value and never by reference. Consequently, a `catch` block which handles a particular type (or class) is equivalent to one which handles references to this type (or class) — furthermore, the `const` keyword is ignored when selecting a handler.

More importantly a `catch` handler for a base class will also catch objects from a derived class. This fact is useful if the exception classes are arranged into a hierarchy — general error processing may be performed in a base class handler whilst more specific processing is possible in a derived class handler. Since `catch` handlers are scanned from top to bottom of the list until a match is found, the handlers for derived classes must precede those for the corresponding base class — the C++ rules for implicit casting of pointer types means that the same is true for handlers which catch pointer types.

Finally, the `...` symbol is used to indicate that a handler will accept any type of exception — such a handler should be last in the list following the `try` block.

As an example, suppose a `DIVIDE_BY_ZERO` class derives from the `MATH_ERROR` class:

```
class DIVIDE_BY_ZERO : public MATH_ERROR {
  DIVIDE_BY_ZERO(void);
};

DIVIDE_BY_ZERO::DIVIDE_BY_ZERO(void) {
  Code = 1001;
}
```

The following arrangement of `catch` handlers is possible:

```
try {
  .
  .
  .
}
catch (DIVIDE_BY_ZERO error) {
  // specific error processing
}
catch (MATH_ERROR error) {
  // general MATH_ERROR processing
}
catch (...) {
  // general error processing
}
```

If a handler cannot be found in the list following the `try` block the exception is passed on to any enclosing `try` block and the process repeats. The same thing happens if an exception is thrown from a `catch` handler — the keyword `throw` on its own rethrows the original exception. When the outermost `try` block is reached and no handler can be found, the program will terminate.

15.4 Unwinding the Stack

The clever thing about exceptions is that they coordinate their activities with the creation and destruction of local objects. Whenever a block statement is exited through the action of throwing an exception any objects local to the block are destroyed. As discussed in section 10.1 local objects are typically stored on the stack and so the process of automatically destroying the local objects is known as unwinding the stack. For example, the OBJECT class defines the following constructor and destructor:

```
OBJECT::OBJECT(void) {
  cout << "Creating Object ...\n";
}

OBJECT::~OBJECT(void) {
  cout << "Destroying Object ...\n";
}
```

The following code demonstrates what happens when an exception is thrown:

```
try {
  OBJECT object;
    .
    .
  int error = 1001;
  throw error;
    .
    .
}
catch (int i) {
  cout << "Error code " << i;
  cout << " caught.\n";
  exit(999);
}
```

The object is destroyed before the exception is caught — the following messages are printed:

```
Creating Object ...
Destroying Object ...
Error code 1001 caught.
```

In particular, the stack is unwound when a function is invoked from within a **try** block and it then proceeds to throw an exception — any local objects created by the function are destroyed before control is passed to an error handler for the **try** block.

15.5 Constructors

Constructors interact with exceptions in a unique way. If an exception is thrown from within a constructor then the object is not considered to be fully constructed — the destructor is not called for the object. For an object with embedded objects the construction process involves two steps:

1. Construct the embedded objects
2. Execute the object's own constructor

If an exception is thrown in either step, the only destructors invoked are those for embedded objects which were fully constructed before the exception was thrown. Similarly for an object of a derived class the construction steps are:

1. Construct embedded objects defined in the base class
2. Execute the object's own base class constructor
3. Construct embedded objects defined in the derived class
4. Execute the object's own derived class constructor

Again if an exception is thrown only fully constructed embedded objects have their destructors invoked — the base class destructor is called only if the base class constructor completed successfully.

A constructor is often used to acquire resources for the object — the destructor will release these resource. For example:

```
OBJECT::OBJECT(void) {
  Storage = (char*) new char[1000];
  if (!Storage) {
    OUT_OF_MEMORY exception;
    throw exception;
  }
}

OBJECT::~OBJECT(void) {
  delete [] Storage;
}
```

Here the OBJECT class acquires one thousand bytes of storage for each object to use. An OUT_OF_MEMORY exception is thrown by the constructor if it cannot acquire its storage — in this case the matching call to the destructor to release the resource becomes unnecessary and indeed never happens.